THE SEPARATION GUIDE

THE SEPARATION GUIDE

KNOW YOUR OPTIONS, TAKE CONTROL, AND GET YOUR LIFE BACK

David Greig, LAWYER

Self-Counsel Press
(a division of)
International Self-Counsel Press Ltd.
USA   Canada

Self-Counsel Press acknowledges the financial support of the Government of Canada through the Canada Book Fund (CBF) for our publishing activities.

First edition: 2011

Library and Archives Canada Cataloguing in Publication

Greig, David

The separation guide / David Greig.

ISBN 978-1-77040-057-3

1. Separation (Law) — Canada. 2. Divorce — Canada. 3. Marriage — Canada. 4. Domestic relations — Canada. I. Title.

HQ838.G74 2010   306.89   C2010-902052-9

Inside Images
Copyright©iStockphoto/Broken Home/Paula Connelly

MIX
Paper from
responsible sources
FSC
www.fsc.org   FSC® C004071

Self-Counsel Press
(a division of)
International Self-Counsel Press Ltd.

1704 North State Street   1481 Charlotte Road
Bellingham, WA 98225   North Vancouver, BC V7J 1H1
USA   Canada

Contents

Samples

Notice to Readers

Laws are constantly changing. Every effort is made to keep this publication as current as possible. However, the author, the publisher, and the vendor of this book make no representations or warranties regarding the outcome or the use to which the information in this book is put and are not assuming any liability for any claims, losses, or damages arising out of the use of this book. The reader should not rely on the author or the publisher of this book for any professional advice. Please be sure that you have the most recent edition.

Introduction

In some Mexican tourist destinations, the Customs and Immigration authorities at the airport use a very low-tech method of deciding which visitors will be searched. As travelers near the exit from the airport, they are required to push a large button adjacent to the exit turnstile. The button controls a mechanical device which illuminates a nearby light randomly. It resembles a big indoor traffic light. The light is watched closely by all. About half of the visitors will quite accidentally trip a green light. Their holiday starts immediately. They pass outside the airport and off to vacation spots in pursuit of happy times. The other half will get a red light. Their fun must wait while the family luggage is searched for contraband.

Marriage is like that. Half of all marriages in North America end in divorce. If you are married now, there's almost a 50 percent chance that some random event which is about to occur will cause your red light to be illuminated. If that light goes on, then, like the unfortunate traveler, you'll soon be victimized by an authority figure who will be looking through your underwear. But it won't be a Mexican Customs officer — it will be your spouse's lawyer. And the lawyer won't be looking for contraband — he or she will be looking for *anything*. Anything at all!

Here in North America, we've been marrying and divorcing with predictable regularity for many decades. You would think that high divorce rates would discourage marriage. Not so. Marriage remains extremely popular. In 2009, the marriage rate for those in the prime reproductive years in the United States was 6.8 per 1,000. The divorce rate? You guessed it: 3.4 per 1,000.

Couples prefer marriage to simple cohabitation. Although half of all married folk once lived with their spouse (in a common-law relationship prior to the wedding), only 9 percent of all couples in childbearing years tend to cohabit in the absence of wedlock. Marriage is still the preferred eventual course.

Interestingly, it's believed that arranged marriages end with divorce rates which are actually slightly lower than the rate for couples who married for love, although there may be cultural explanations for that. We don't really know, although we believe that marrying for love is just as risky as marrying for other reasons.

Similarly interesting is the fact that second-timers seem to fare better. The divorce rate amongst persons who have married more than once is about half that of the general population. It may be because being a good spouse is learned behavior. Perhaps spouses learn to get along better with each successive relationship. Or maybe second- and third-timers simply die before they have a chance to divorce. Nobody knows for sure.

What we do know is that marriage can be a wonderful thing, or it can be hell. There are probably more awful divorce stories than there are happy marriage stories. Everyone knows a tale about how a marriage failed and ended in disaster, causing immeasurable financial loss, trauma for children, and other miscellaneous and irreparable damage. The tales are widespread, and some are even true.

Just recently, someone asked me for some advice. I suppose he had heard from another person that I was a lawyer, and so he figured he'd tell me about his thoughts on the law. This happens quite a bit, actually. Even though I get the routine with some frequency, I must confess that I'm still amazed every time somebody decides to share his or her law story with me. It's funny, really — I never want to discuss my sore knee with an acquaintance who's a surgeon!

Anyway, the fellow began by explaining to me that he was aware that all men get the "short end of the stick" in divorces, and he wondered if I knew about that. Not actually interested in my answer, he began to wonder (out loud) how I could bear to work in such a corrupt system. Soon, he was telling me about the source of his knowledge (he'd been divorced twice) and he explained that his second wife "got the mine" while he "got the shaft"! He looked at me as though I must surely know the story; I think I was expected to laugh as he said it jokingly. The point is that everybody has a divorce story. Some are funny, some are sad, but few are intrinsically good or happy stories.

Despite all that, people marry and divorce with predictable frequency. The success and failure of relationships over time has been one of the most prominent and steadfast features of life in North America for at least 50 years. Even though most aspects of our culture have become almost unrecognizable in that same period, the basic concept of marriage remains virtually unchanged.

This point can be easily understood by thinking about how every feature of our culture and economy has changed. Compare the present-day world to almost any preexisting period. Think what music sounded like at the end of the seventeenth century and compare that to digitally enhanced rap. Think about the way Mickey Mouse appeared in the first Disney show, and then contrast that with the computer-generated creatures in *Shrek*. Consider the changes to the culture around storytelling and fiction in the days of Shakespearean theater versus film in the twenty-first century. Step outside of culture and think about science and technology from 8-tracks to iPods, carrier pigeons to cell phones, bloodletting to genetics, and horse-drawn carriages to hybrid vehicles. Every aspect of our world has changed radically. However, attend a friend's wedding and you will immediately see something that really hasn't changed lately at all.

Despite all our cultural diversity, the advancement of science and the arts, revolutionary technological and massive ideological changes, marriage is one aspect of our North American way of life which remains almost completely untouched.

Think about the last wedding you attended. It's likely the bride wore white and the men wore black. Everybody met on a Saturday, at the church. The parties signed papers, exchanged rings, feasted together, shared speeches, kissed in public, and then the couple went on a honeymoon. It's pretty much the same in Fort Worth in 2010 as what you'll see in any version of Robin Hood. With no disrespect to newlywed lovers, almost all weddings are the same.

Marriage itself has not changed. Yet our perceptions about good and bad marriages have. True, those changes have not been the changes that we've seen in science, technology, and communications — but there have been changes.

For instance, loveless marriage is now almost universally considered intolerable. Spouses leave relationships for more money, better sex, less arguing, or just because they need a change. Husbands and wives seem to "check out" of a relationship more willingly, more easily, and more swiftly, and yet overall divorce rates remain surprisingly static.

Most significantly, the available statistical data shows that the process for obtaining a divorce, separating assets, dealing with children's issues, and dividing liabilities and responsibilities remains relatively constant. We still argue, posture, negotiate, hire lawyers, negotiate some more, settle, or proceed to trial. We do so largely with the same systems and processes that existed when my dad practiced law in the late 1950s. Sure, some attitudes and principles of law have changed, but overall, the system remains surprisingly steadfast. Some would say it is still costly, cruel, and inconvenient.

This book is no valiant attempt to change all that. Better and smarter lawyers and jurists have change in mind, and many law societies, governments, and educators are now working on modifications to the system that will improve, streamline, and simplify divorce laws and processes. The program for change is underway, and it is likely to continue indefinitely.

Meanwhile, as that work continues, couples continue to marry, separate, and divorce. They need and deserve information about how to think, act, and behave in the process of separation. They need to understand that there are ways to increase the likelihood that the separation itself will be survivable.

This is what this book is about. Here, we're going to explore a better approach to separation and divorce, and encourage parties to calmly negotiate a sensible resolution of their dispute without heartache and bloodshed. Done correctly, a separation and divorce can be an empowering, invigorating, and even liberating event.

Much of the information in this book will be applicable to common-law separations as well.

An Important Note about This Book

I have been practicing family law in Vancouver, British Columbia, for 25 years. During that time, I have met and worked with all kinds of clients, in all kinds of family situations. Some of the cases I've worked on have been unbelievable, while others follow a predictable pattern.

Along the way, I have been educated by the process and by the clients. I believe that what I have learned can save separating couples time, money, and heartache.

Some of the people I have worked with have been notorious and famous, while others have been quiet and humble. Many of my clients struggled with horrific spousal abuse, fraud, and secrecy, while others left relationships for financial, sexual, or other reasons. I have occasionally seen clients separate quietly, in peace, and part company as friends. They, truly, are the lucky ones.

Very often, drugs and alcohol are at the center of the trouble. Other times, it's gambling, dishonesty, or other worrisome behavior that brings the relationship to an end. However, completely "normal," balanced, stable, hardworking, and honest people also fall out of love. Sometimes, despite the best efforts of well-intentioned parties, spousal relationships end, and former lovers part ways.

I have seen this, in my career, thousands of times. Seeing it over and over again has taught me nothing about love and marriage. However, the specific stories I have heard and handled have taught me something about family law. What I've learned is something that cannot be taught in law school and isn't easily absorbed from everyday life. The lesson that I have learned, and which I hope to share in this book, is that separation and divorce can be a good experience.

This is a book about a process that can lead to happiness *from* separation and divorce. It is about how parties can negotiate a solution to their matrimonial or spousal separation on their own. The book explains how and when expert help can and should be obtained to assist in the process; however, it encourages the parties to do the heavy lifting and most of the work.

I am writing this book to share the lessons I've learned and to explain how the process works. From time to time, as a part of that explanation, I expect to tell you about examples and cases I've handled which have some educational value. All of the stories must, however, remain private, due to solicitor-client privilege. I can, however, tell readers about known facts, reported cases, and other "stories" so long as the privilege is protected. To do that, I must change the names, of course, and sometimes alter some of the facts to keep identities secret.

Sometimes, the language of the examples may appear and sound slightly sexist. I mean no disrespect by this, and apologize in advance for any insult I may cause. The biological fact is that so far, only women bear children. The social and historical corollary of this seems to be that there is a difference between women and men in the law, in respect to children's issues. Maybe that's good or maybe that's bad. Maybe that will all change soon. I don't know. For now, to be brief, I have used examples that I think best illustrate real principles concerning separation and children's topics, and in the process I may use some generalizations that could conceivably appear sexist. Sorry, that is not my intention.

This book is not about the specific laws that apply in your state, province, country, or region. There are good (and bad) sources available on the Internet and in print which can assist you with understanding the governing legal principles in your jurisdiction. You can obtain that advice on the Internet, in your library, or from various legal clinics, lawyers, and other resources in your community. This book won't help with the particular laws that apply to your case.

Instead, here I offer advice and information about the process for negotiating a mutually satisfactory end to your separation. That resolution is going to be achieved by communicating with your spouse. You may or may not be able to have that communication directly. Perhaps it will be in writing, with a friend, or through a mediator. It doesn't really matter how you resolve your issues, as long as they are resolved in the absence of litigation.

Before you finalize or sign anything, I will remind you (several times) that you must obtain independent legal advice about the deal you are making. Getting proper, competent, and local legal advice about your situation is imperative, and it is imperative you get that advice before you sign or sell anything.

I believe this book can be helpful because although every divorce is unique, there are common themes and principles at play in all cases. Knowing these common themes from my experience in law has provided me with the opportunity to explain so that newcomers to separation can avoid common mistakes that others have made. At the same time, I can describe some of the positive steps that can be taken to increase the likelihood of early resolution of the case. I'll also explain how to discourage costly rancor and acrimonious litigation.

Knowing something about how other family cases have ended badly or resulted in lengthy and costly litigation can help you avoid a similar fate. Having that knowledge at the outset is important because the litigation process can be self-perpetuating. Once parties start down the litigation path, it's often difficult to get off that path.

When a dispute escalates due to litigation, or because the parties simply don't know how to get out of the bickering cycle, there are several options and methodologies available to overcome the blockage. Some are better than others. Each of the options is easy to see from the outside, but sometimes impossible to imagine for the participants at the center of the dispute. It is for that reason that parties in a dispute need to get advice from outside the dispute. Referring a friend or family member to a lawyer, mediator, arbitrator, or even a book takes some courage. It's not easy to tell a buddy that he or she needs help.

Legal rules and principles about practice, procedure, and substantive law vary throughout North America. The laws that govern divorce and separation in Alaska have no application in British Columbia or California. Having said that, the same basic issues and disputes arise in most cases, and do so with repetitive frustration, over and over again. This book can help you avoid making those same patterned mistakes. It can help you reach a settlement that is timely, inexpensive, and survivable. As you continue on in your reading, keep in mind that regional (jurisdictional) changes and subtle differences in the law may require careful consideration.

1

The Roles of the Lawyer and the Litigant

When I graduated from law school in 1986, the economy in my hometown was poor. The real estate market had just struggled through a major adjustment, unemployment was high, and interest rates were creating market uncertainty. It was not a great time to be starting a new career.

In my case, that career started at a small local firm in which the partners were friendly and the atmosphere was collegial. I wasn't planning on getting rich immediately, and so financial issues weren't really on my mind. The staff was great, and everyone was welcoming. Since the firm was already established, I was given the opportunity to try almost anything that came in the door. I tried my hand at several different kinds of law. Sometimes, I would land a criminal case or a construction law matter. I even incorporated a few companies and learned a bit about real estate law.

Within a short time, however, I discovered that the interesting thing about the practice of law had almost nothing to do with "law." The principles and rules of the work were actually quite dull. Instead, what was interesting was the clients — the people who had real problems and needed help. They had wild stories, interesting lives, and complex challenges. I soon learned to enjoy being a professional who was able to help real people solve real problems in their lives. It made me feel useful and satisfied, and so for that selfish reason I persisted.

In those years, while there was no shortage of work, there was a shortage of high-paying work. The huge "shopping center" solicitor cases and the major-loss car crash claims were few and far between. Those cases paid big money, but there was stiff competition for them, and I was new to the business. I soon found, however, that even though the big sought-after cases were in short supply, there was an abundance of family law cases and claims, and very few lawyers who were keen to do that work.

Now, 25 years later, the world has changed radically, but this aspect of the practice of law remains unchanged. Today, perhaps more than ever, there are thousands of families all across the continent with a variety of family law problems. And believe it or not, there's a shortage of competent, caring family law lawyers who are willing to help.

Maybe young lawyers don't go into the practice deliberately because divorce law isn't really all that sexy. Aside from some interesting fictional insights offered long ago when *L.A. Law* romanticized the glitz and glamour of divorce practice, there's never really been any doubt that divorce law is the least popular kind of work in the field. Really, no law student lies awake at night dreaming about being an advocate in a custody case. Instead, the law student's dreams are focused on constitutional change in the Supreme Court, or winning a huge environmental challenge, or freeing an innocent person. Arguing over the daycare arrangements for Sally Smith just isn't that glitzy. Tom Cruise would never have to do a case like that in a movie!

Moreover, if you are a young lawyer with $100,000 in student loans and a group of friends who have already been in the labor market for four or five years, you need to practice in a remunerative area, and recoup your expenses.

Although many films and series have depicted legal careers as easy pathways to exciting cases and the effortless accumulation of unimaginable wealth, anyone on the reality side of the room knows that family law is not like that. Most divorce lawyers work long, hard hours in difficult circumstances, with challenging clients, and earn a modest income. It's a difficult job that requires special skills. Sometimes, it just doesn't pay well. As a result, it's not seen as an attractive kind of practice.

For that reason, family law is underpopulated by lawyers. That may be one reason why many litigants choose to represent themselves — there just aren't large numbers of available divorce lawyers around, and those that are skilled and experienced are not inexpensive. Really, it's the law of supply and demand.

As well, because family law cases are expensive and seem to arise at a time when a family is already experiencing economic (and emotional) turmoil, many spouses facing family law cases do so without any legal help whatsoever. It's not that they want to act for themselves — they simply do not have the money for counsel. The erosion of legal aid for family law clients has caused even more warring spouses to act alone.

This trend cannot be seriously challenged. More and more, separating spouses are finding it impossible to pay lawyers for help. This creates challenges for society generally, and for judges and the development of legal precedent.

The number of unrepresented divorce litigants has been on the rise for some time, and in my jurisdiction at least, it seems unlikely to change any time soon. The result is that many family law cases are decided by judges who have not heard all the facts or all the arguments, simply because the parties are self-represented and lack the training necessary to explain their side of the story in a convincing and persuasive way. Not having an experienced divorce lawyer on your side can have disastrous effects which may last forever.

In the years that I have been doing this job, I have seen many self-represented litigants. Some have been surprisingly professional and persuasive. Most, sadly, lack the skills and objectivity to do a good job with their own case. You don't need to be foolish to miss facts and destroy a case. Some very clever people have managed that.

By acting for yourself in litigation (and sometimes even during difficult negotiations) you can miscalculate. What matters in law or fact can be overshadowed by your concern over an insignificant detail. In court, presenting your own argument can often prove disastrous. You may, in the process, alienate the judge or destroy your own argument. When you act for yourself, you take the "arguing lawyer" who acts as a buffer out of the equation. Usually, your proximity to the sensitive issues and your complete lack of objectivity is enough to ruin your chance of a fair hearing.

What is really unfortunate about self-represented litigants is that most of them don't understand enough about the system to appreciate which tasks they can safely do on their own and which tasks truly require legal advice.

Consider the following examples:

- Most lawyers will perform task-based assignments, and are willing to work on a piecemeal basis. Some call this "unbundling," meaning the lawyer does not act for the client generally, or on all matters, but is only retained for a specific purpose. For instance, sometimes I am hired to review a separation agreement (and "fix it"), or for the purpose of opposing one part of a court case. Other times, I'm retained only to conduct a trial. In this way, the client has the benefit of counsel for part of the case, but does not suffer the expense of a general retainer.

- Some of the work that lawyers and their staff perform (and charge for) is work that the litigant can do without any risk and without any legal knowledge. For instance, the client can organize documentary materials, provide witness summaries (outlining the personal particulars of each helpful witness and providing a summary of what the witness will say, etc.). This can and should be done by the party — not the lawyer.

- Another alternative is to retain a lawyer to give advice, but to conduct the hearings yourself. I recently did this on a case involving a local father, and it worked wonderfully. The father was a sensible man and had a reasonably strong case. He was quite able to conduct the trial himself and only needed guidance with the procedure and the legal principles. He retained me for general advice, and I talked with him a half dozen times before the trial and every day during the trial. He succeeded, as I thought he would, in his claim for custody. By acting for himself, he probably saved $25,000. This is a risky prospect, and should be reserved only for certain scenarios, but it can always be considered and kept in mind as one option.

What I am suggesting here is that there are alternatives to the traditional lawyer/client relationship. It's not an "all or nothing" proposition. Each case is different. What worked for your friend may not work for you. Many of my most reasonable clients would be disasters in court and would be easy prey for the most junior lawyer. Other clients can do most of the work themselves and need me only for specific tasks. Still others can negotiate and settle a case, and want me only to review their agreement or assist in drafting it. Gone are the days when every separating spouse needs $25,000 and an aggressive lawyer.

Still, understanding the concepts and putting them into play are two very different things. In order to achieve your separation objectives without breaking the bank and without nasty litigation, you need to be committed to the process. You need to understand that if you play your cards correctly, you can have a "happy divorce." It's not a result that is available to everyone, but you will never know unless you try.

1. Similar Cases; Extremely Different Results

I was quite a distance into my career before I realized that the concept of a "good" separation or divorce was realistic.

The event unveiled itself rather innocuously, on a rainy Tuesday morning in November. I had started early that morning, as I usually do, preparing for appointments, upcoming court cases, and answering electronic and snail mail. At about 8:00 a.m., my first appointment arrived. The client, a pleasant looking, middle-aged woman with a small briefcase and a quiet demeanor introduced herself and came to sit in my office. I'll call her "Mrs. G."

She described her circumstances calmly and carefully, and explained that she had separated a year earlier. She told me about her two children, her financial situation, her husband's career, and her aspirations for the future. Mrs. G then described how she wanted a serious and aggressive lawyer who could "handle" her husband — someone who wouldn't be afraid to stand up to him. The client told me that her husband was a financial bully, had several good lawyers and accountants at his disposal, and she warned me that he could put up a good fight. In essence, she wanted me to "undress" him and in the process obtain a favorable order or settlement. Her objectives were clear — she was sure that spousal support was her entitlement and she wanted more than half the family assets. She then flattered me with a comment about how she had heard good things about me, and turned the discussion to fees, the time line for progress, and other matters. Throughout, she was clear, concise, and businesslike.

I kept notes, asked questions, and gave some advice to Mrs. G. At the end of the interview (about 70 minutes later), she gave me a check for the retainer and left the office apparently pleased. I dictated a memo about the facts, organized the file materials and the documents she'd left, and then asked my legal assistant to open a file. My final instructions were marked in the right-hand margin at the bottom of the fifth page, which said, "Litigation matter — client wants divorce, custody, and spousal support, *plus 75 percent of the assets*." I then went on with the rest of my morning, and dealt with a variety of other issues.

After lunch, I had another appointment with a second potential female client. Again, I introduced myself in the lobby and escorted the lady to my office. This client looked and sounded somewhat like Mrs. G. As her story was presented, I was surprised to find that, in fact, some of the basic family information was similar to the story Mrs. G had told. Here, there were also two kids, an ambitious and well-off husband, and concerns about custody, money, and the future. At the outset of the interview, I knew the new client's first name only, and used it judiciously, but when it came time to get the critical and essential information necessary to open the file, I asked for her surname. As she pronounced it and then spelled it out for me, I was astonished to find that there was but one letter which distinguished her name from Mrs. G. Not only were the facts and stories strikingly similar, they had almost the same name! What a coincidence!

My second client was Mrs. B, and she too (like Mrs. G) needed a lawyer. She and her husband had been negotiating for some time, but they were apparently at a stalemate. Although Mrs. B had hoped for an amicable resolve, the battle lines appeared to be drawn. She too was resigned to litigation and hoped I could help.

Mrs. B did not, however, tell me that she wanted litigation. Instead, she asked if there was anything I could do — "even a last-ditch settlement offer" — that might result in a friendly resolution. She was quite sure that her husband would not budge or reconsider the offers, but she asked me to try one more time notwithstanding. I could tell she was tired and anxious and felt weakened, but still there was hope.

I told her I would do my best, and she seemed somewhat reassured. Mrs. B left me a retainer, and I prepared to open the file and provide instructions to staff. This time, however, the final instructions at the bottom of page five said, "Client convinced it's hopeless but wants to try last-ditch settlement offer as per instructions above. Try letter to husband before and give it one last shot."

After the Mrs. B file had been opened, I drafted that settlement letter to the husband. I did so in nonconfrontational language, and described some concessions and options that the client had explained to me. I asked the husband to give the proposal careful consideration, particularly since it seemed likely that litigation would follow if we were unable to settle soon. I asked him to talk to other lawyers, and I gave him the names of some colleagues. I expected the letter to achieve nothing, but I gave it a try. It was what the client wanted.

The next day, I prepared the court pleadings and documents necessary to start the lawsuit in the Mrs. G versus Mr. G case. A process server was contacted, and the stage was set.

The Mrs. G case finished about six months ago. In the end, I extracted a judgment that was favorable to the client, and managed to obtain an order for spousal support and a significant reapportionment of family assets. It was a substantial victory — she had been a good witness and we had done a good job. The client was relatively sympathetic and the husband behaved poorly. The evidence had come out perfectly, and we were lucky with the judge who was appointed to the case. Overall, it was a fantastic outcome.

The case had, however, been costly. The legal fees were several tens of thousands of dollars, and the case had occupied a great deal of time. There were several experts, some nastiness in the evidence, and more than a few tears along the way. It had been an exhausting experience for the client, and even though she obtained the desired result, the price paid had been very high indeed. In the end, it had been an emotional bloodbath for the parties, although we had achieved for the client exactly what she wanted.

In my final meeting with Mrs. G, I gave her copies of the order of the court, the documents she'd need, my account, and the various other key aspects of the file materials. She was grateful enough, and paid the bill in full. Still, she seemed oddly unhappy and unsettled. Unable to extract a heartfelt confession from her as to the exact source of the discomfort, I left her and wished her the best, hoping that her world would be better from the service we provided. My job was done. Or so I thought.

Mrs. G returned a few short months later. She had problems with access and support. The checks were late and the ex-husband was not showing up for the access he had fought so hard for and been granted. There were verbal altercations at pick-up and drop-off, and he was using her tardy support payments as a way of "getting back."

In about four months, the ex-Mrs. G had been back into the office three times, on each occasion asking for help. I called counsel for the ex-husband, until he removed himself from the case. Then I called the husband. He seemed okay on the phone, but always had a long explanation. I wrote letters. He ignored me. Within about five months of the trial, we were back in court again, on a motion about support and access. We got our way on the support issue, but the court reminded us that they could not force Mr. G to use the access, and the judge made ancillary orders about how canceled access would require advance notice. Still, the trouble continued.

I did what I could, but the client's insatiable appetite for continued litigation was too much, and I told her so. I reminded her that just before trial, we had been close to settlement, and that the husband's offer was quite fair. I had suggested she take it, even though the support was a little "light." She had refused, insisting on trial. I had said that a support settlement (paid on time, because it's agreeable) is better than a court-ordered settlement for a higher amount, paid irregularly and begrudgingly. She didn't recall that conversation. She demanded to get back in court. I said I thought she needed to consider her options. Shortly thereafter, I received a request from another lawyer for the file to be transferred. Mrs. G had found someone new to fight the good fight. The war continues to rage.

After that file was transferred out, I left the office, heading out for a quiet lunch. I found myself wondering if in fact Mrs. G ever really, truly wanted closure at all. It occurred to me that perhaps what she really wanted was the fight itself — that perhaps she needed a hard-fought battle with the man who had done her wrong, and that she hadn't wanted it all to end with the judgment. She found ongoing complaints and topics of concern because she really had not finished with Mr. G, and she wanted me to prolong the entire conflict and contact. Maybe it was her way of maintaining some control, or some semblance of a relationship with the man who once loved her and let her down. Then, at that very moment, as these thoughts were swirling around in my mind, I rounded a corner deep in thought and ran almost headlong into Mrs. B.

"Sorry!" I shouted, simultaneously surprised at my own recklessness and the sight of my former client. Mrs. B stood before me, shopping bags in hand, looking so very different from the way she had appeared when I last saw her many months earlier. Now she looked bright, happy, and full of energy.

We exchanged some simple pleasantries, and then I asked her how she was (in a serious and businesslike way). She took a big breath and looked at me, unsure whether I was a friend, previous business associate, or former lawyer. After a moment of apparent consideration, she said she was "honestly, very happy."

Her manner of speaking made the comment redundant. It was obvious to anyone that Mrs. B (now going by a different name) was clearly happy and content by any measure. She looked good.

We stepped out of the main concourse to talk. She told me how things had "come together" for her in the aftermath of resolution. She said that when her case ended, she wasn't sure if she'd be able to manage, but she had some remaining confidence that stayed with her even though she had felt vulnerable.

She said she remembered that I had told her an average settlement was twice as good as a great victory at trial. She remarked that her ex-husband, once a fierce combatant, was actually being almost easy to deal with, and had been cooperative on several children's issues lately. He had found a new woman, and my former client found it surprisingly easy to communicate with this new woman.

She was glad that the case had settled, and even more pleased that the resolution had been achieved without huge expense or acrimony. She seemed genuinely happy and settled. Although she had not recovered everything she wanted, she had found some peace and had moved on. Getting perfect financial justice had, in the end, proven to be relatively unimportant. For her, the settlement and eventual divorce had been invigorating and uplifting, and she and the kids were happier than they had ever been.

As I walked away, I began to think about her happiness, and the very different and very unhappy experience that Mrs. G had gone through. Although no two cases are ever the same, I began to consider the similarities of the issues, the topics that were argued, and the results obtained. As I did, I realized that while there were some obvious differences between the two families, the parallels were remarkable. Mrs. G and Mrs. B had nearly identical cases and claims, and almost opposite experiences and results. I started to wonder why that was so.

My thinking about this issue is primarily what has led to the development of this book. For, in considering the cases side by side, I came to realize that the factor that brought Mrs. G such misery and Mrs. B such calm was not the process itself, the minutiae of the detail, or any other difference or distinction; it was that a fundamentally different approach had been taken from the outset. Mrs. B came to my office with a desire to settle and resolve the dispute in a non-acrimonious way. She did so understanding that litigation might result, but committed to avoiding that (probably because she knew it was undesirable, unaffordable, and impractical). Mrs. G, on the other hand, started the process wanting blood, expecting justice, and demanding litigation. Hell-bent for some inarticulate and insatiable objective, she could not be satisfied even when the litigation went exactly as she had wanted. No fair or even generous judgment could satisfy her desires because fairness was not the objective.

The lesson learned from these two files has taught me three things that are worth knowing and sharing:

- When it comes to negotiating a settlement, **never say never**. Do not leave the world of negotiation because you believe that the case will never settle. Sure, it may settle even after you start the litigation, but once litigation has commenced, the stakes are much higher and the sensitivities are extremely heightened.

- When you are negotiating and trying to settle, you must never believe that litigation is a practical alternative — **litigation is not a reasonable option**. It may be absolutely unavoidable in some cases (when there's violence or hidden assets), but for most separating spouses, litigation just doesn't make sense.

- **Remember that you may be happier if you settle and miserable even if you win a lawsuit.**

2

Understanding the Situation — Litigation May Not Be Necessary

 Litigation is a process that is designed to serve a very special and very unusual person. The ideal litigant is someone who —

- has genuinely tried all other dispute-resolution options and failed for reasons which cannot be remedied,

- has plenty of money for the process and for the lawyers,

- is strong, and

- can afford to lose.

There are two basic litigation processes: the *inquisitorial* system and the *adversarial* system.

The inquisitorial system is where the judge or adjudicator is charged with the duty of inquiring into the event at issue, finding out what happened, and determining the facts. The best example of an inquisitorial tribunal in our lives is the process that occurs after a major tragedy (e.g., a plane or train crash), where a panel of experts is assembled to investigate and find out what went wrong. Sometimes, it's conducted as a coroner's inquiry. Other times, it's a government-appointed body that is gathered to get to the bottom of a particular tragedy, to find out what occurred and what can be done in the future to avoid a similar event. The purpose is not to find fault and levy blame.

The adversarial system has a very different objective and a very different process. The adversarial system is the typical court process that we all think about when we remember old *Perry Mason* episodes or recall scenes from the movie *Judgment at Nuremburg*.

Our litigation system is adversarial. That means that our litigation proceeds on the premise that if each party puts his or her best case forward and has a chance at a hearty cross examination, the truth will spill out and the judge can then assign fault or blame and fix everything. In the process, of course, a few heads are likely to roll. In family law, since we're not really interested in knowing who caused the breakdown of the marriage, the purpose of the adversarial system is clearly misplaced. Why a marriage collapsed just doesn't matter.

Because our system is imperfect, and not really designed for divorce law issues, other options have developed over the years. Now, in North America, there exist many alternatives to litigation. Some are inexpensive, speedy, and low-conflict. Others (i.e., arbitration) are similar to the existing legal system, but have cost and accessibility advantages. Some systems work for some people, while other parties simply cannot find peace no matter what they do. Regardless, the point is that if you are separating, you need to know about the alternatives, and you need to remember that full-blown litigation is, truly, the last option you should consider. Litigation should occur only when every other alternative has failed.

One reason for this is that even the strongest and wealthiest clients find the litigation process far too costly from both an emotional and a fiscal perspective. Some know that at the outset, and wisely resolve issues before the fight becomes too entangled. Others learn the lesson too late, and only set their sights on settlement after huge expenses and nasty affidavits. Even if you are rich, it should be remembered that litigation wastes money, and that's money that can be better used for other purposes (e.g., children, counseling, luxuries, or charity).

A litigant must be internally strong, too. In order to effectively withstand cross examination, the taunting nature of the process, and all the twists and turns and uncertainties of a lawsuit, you need strength and confidence. Many who outwardly appear to have that strength overestimate their stamina and resources, and discover too late that litigation is simply overwhelming.

If you must litigate because there is no alternative, a lawyer can help you get ready for the process and guide you through the challenges. The following chapters describe what steps you can take before and during a lawsuit to improve your situation and increase the likelihood that you'll be a good witness. If you must testify so be it; the point here is that most separating spouses have choices to make. Surprisingly, a majority still choose litigation.

Although the horrors of litigation cannot be overstated, every week I have clients *insist* on proceeding to court in search of justice. It's almost as if hiring a lawyer and starting a lawsuit is a badge of bravado or a demonstration of strength. Very often I am able to dissuade these clients through calm discussion about the risks, expenses, and process associated with that. Often it's hopeless — some people insist on going to court.

Sometimes, it's absolutely necessary to go to court, but it's rare. The vast majority of the cases that are argued in court might have been resolved if only the parties had remained committed to the process a little longer, or gone with slightly different approaches.

I think one reason why people almost automatically head to court during separation is that they lack confidence about whether the dispute can be resolved by any other method. They don't know what the options are, and expect a conflict, so they want to "get started." Having a case up and running reminds them that the relationship has ended and that they are doing something about it.

Some folks even believe that there is a tactical advantage to being the first litigant. They believe that being a defendant is a disadvantage. That's untrue, of course, but I wonder how many lawsuits have been started with that thought in mind.

Many litigants get into the courts because they assume that their spouse is foolishly stubborn, won't settle, can't understand logic, and won't listen to his or her lawyer or mediator. That kind of thinking may cost thousands of dollars and a great deal of anguish.

Having said all that, there exist numerous examples of cases where the absolute fear of lawyers and litigation has proven disastrous. There are circumstances where legal advice is worth its weight in gold. You just have to know when, where, and how to use a lawyer.

Several years ago, I had a man come to see me for a free initial interview. He told me his entire story, and I gave him some advice and ideas about various options. He was grateful for the information and left.

About a month later he called again. He wanted another appointment, so I agreed to meet a second time. We talked further, and I answered a series of specific questions. At the end, I told him that he must get proper legal advice before signing anything, and I warned him about the risks of homemade agreements. I did not believe he was being suitably cautious, and I was worried about his rush to resolution. He seemed absolutely focused on getting a deal even if it was a bad deal. Troubling, too, was the fact that he wanted a great deal of free advice about tricky concepts, and he wanted to pay nothing for it. This reminded me of the adage about being penny wise and pound foolish. I made a note of this, and told him that there would be a fee for the next meeting.

I didn't hear from him until a year later. At that point, he wanted another free consultation, this time about the divorce. I apparently forgot that he had already milked me for tons of free advice, and so I agreed to a short third and final meeting.

He made the appointment and showed up for the last bit of free information. We exchanged pleasantries, and I asked him if he had resolved matters with his wife. He said he had, and proudly announced that he'd done everything himself. I congratulated him, but reminded him that I had told him on both prior meetings that he must see a lawyer before signing anything. He said yes, he remembered that, but was confident he hadn't needed counsel and said he really didn't want to spend money on lawyers. He had heard what I told him, but insisted that he knew what he was doing. He then proceeded to tell me that in resolving matters with his spouse, they had agreed to share the registered mutual fund portfolio.

In Canada, where I live and work, separating spouses can divide a registered savings portfolio (which is a tax deductible savings instrument) without incurring any income tax. To obtain this benefit and insulate themselves from tax, however, the deal must be contained in a written separation agreement and accompanied by a form (T2220 E). If that's not done, the transaction triggers tax, payable immediately.

The man didn't know that. He hadn't asked me about it, didn't tell me he planned to do it, didn't ask anyone else, and didn't think it was important to find out. More importantly, he didn't see counsel before signing the agreement. Not knowing about the tax benefits of the law, he cashed out his fund and divided the spoils.

At the time, the husband and wife had about $200,000 in this registered savings portfolio. When the fund was cashed in, the liability for tax was triggered, and the government scooped about $60,000. The husband and wife then shared the remains (about $70,000 each) and went their merry ways.

By saving the $500 I would have charged him, the man and his separating wife needlessly gave away about $60,000 to the tax department. Had either of them sought basic legal advice, the fund could have been divided *in specie*, meaning there would have been no tax payable. Nothing!

For this man, the desire to save a few hundred dollars in legal fees cost, quite literally, $60,000. That's an example of a case where a little advice goes a long way.

However, many people regularly overpay lawyers for work and services that are either not necessary or not helpful. In saying that, I'm not suggesting that lawyers are dishonest with clients about work that needs to be done. Very often in my own practice I will recommend clients against taking a particular course of action, only to have them insist that I do their bidding. Although I don't enjoy working with clients who won't take my advice, at the end of the day I have to remember that the client calls the shots. As long as the instructions do not involve something improper or unlawful, it's not really my place to demand that all clients do exactly as I command. That's not really how the relationship works.

Still, from time to time, I have to put my foot down. At this point in my career, I actually do that with greater frequency, sometimes based on principle. For instance, I rarely engage in custody litigation except in special circumstances because I have a personal belief that the process is simply too destructive. The exceptions would include cases of genuine alienation, violence and abuse, and real danger. I don't accept retainers for cases where the parents are simply fighting over the kids on the basis that one parent is "better" than the other.

I'm also not interested in acting for clients who lie to me, won't pay child support, or expect me, as their lawyer, to prove a fact which is unimportant in law, such as adultery. However, that's just me.

What I see, with some frequency, are clients who have wasted money on lawyers. These would include spouses who have deposited a big retainer with a lawyer, and then instructed the lawyer to "process the divorce." Sometimes, equally vague and ridiculous instructions such as "do your best."

I know this happens because I often encounter counsel on the other side of a case who is unaware of exactly what their client wants. As I write this paragraph right now, I am handling a case that is set for trial in three months. We have had several days of discoveries (what most Americans would call depositions) and a few pretrial motions. The case has been going on for about a year. During that time, I have written to opposing counsel three times asking for a response to our offer, a counterproposal, or anything resembling a reply, but I have heard nothing. It is all quite exasperating.

I know that the other party has already paid a little more than $15,000 in legal fees so far, and is probably about to spend a similar amount over the next few months. I suspect the amount that we're arguing about (the "quantum" in issue, and the amount which separates our clients) is $40,000 to $80,000. It may be that if I could encourage the opposing party to simply respond with an offer or counteroffer, I could encourage my client to settle, but I can't. I cannot negotiate with myself.

Worse still, I know that the other side will soon be forced to describe the demand, because at the start of the trial, the judge is going to ask.

In this case, I suspect that opposing counsel is well retained and simply allowing her client to call the shots. The client doesn't know exactly what she wants, because she (like Mrs. G, in the example in Chapter 1) is really pursuing something other than a solution — she wants blood, or justice, or some other ill-defined objective. Sadly, none of those can be achieved through litigation.

What should really be happening is this: The opposing lawyer should sit down with the client and have a heart-to-heart and say something like this:

We're now at a point in this lawsuit where we know enough about the facts to respond to the offer that's on the table. We should do that. I have done everything I can for you. You and I know that there's a range of possible outcomes here. If I do a brilliant job, I can obtain for you a resolution that is beneficial to you and within that range. I cannot, however, change your spouse's personality, get *you all of the assets, or perform miracles. Your spouse offered to pay you $80,000 for your claims. I know you want more. Your case may be worth more, but it's not worth $150,000. Let's talk about a response now. It is time to find out if we can settle. If we don't settle now, I'm going to have to explain your position to the judge in a short while so we might as well know that now.*

Sometimes, that is a conversation that can and should occur at the outset of the retainer. Maybe the discussion cannot be so pointed and direct at the start of the solicitor/client relationship, but something similar can and should occur. This is what I mean when I say that I believe that clients waste money on lawyers. If you don't know what you want or expect at the outset, how can you provide proper instructions to the lawyer? That's like getting in the car to go for a drive, but not having any idea where you want to go or if you have enough cash to get there.

I know that it's often impractical for lawyers and clients to have settlement instructions at the beginning of the retainer. Quite often, the basic facts about the case are not known. A party cannot be expected to give settlement instructions if the issues aren't identified, the facts are unclear, and the options have not been explored. Giving settlement instructions and clear directions early on may not be possible.

Still, in the vast majority of cases, the client knows enough at the very first interview to give directions. Most spouses don't know the precise fair market value of the home in which they live, but they have some idea. Similarly, they may not be intimately familiar with every detail of the savings portfolio, but they know where to find out (usually, with a phone call). After all, it's their life that's at the center of the case, and most of the facts that the lawyer needs to know can be ascertained in that first meeting. There may need to be subsequent phone calls or inquiries for details later, but the big picture can be learned quite simply in an hour or so.

That's not the case, of course, if there are safety issues, hidden assets, or other special considerations. In those cases, information gathering may be involved, and the legal issues complex. In most separations, however, the basic information — the basic story — is actually quite straightforward. In such circumstances, it's quite possible at the first interview to form a general idea about where the settlement discussions should be headed. If that's not possible, the discussion should occur as soon thereafter as possible, in order to ensure that counsel and the client are on the same page, and in order to focus the legal work.

Too often that appears not to happen until after countless hours of legal work have been done. At that point, the parties have incurred legal expenses and become positioned in their views, and settlement becomes more difficult.

In most cases, it's important to know what you want and expect at the outset. It's important to think about those objectives before you commit resources to the exercise. It may also be important to know what the law permits. You should know what you are entitled to before you provide final settlement instructions. Saying to the lawyer "all I want is what I'm entitled to" is almost certain to lead to big legal bills, delay, and frustration. Know what your rights are, but seek relief that matters. And always keep an eye on settlement.

There are, of course, exceptions. As I explain in Chapter 4, if there is oppression, violence, or dishonesty in a relationship, it may be necessary to litigate, or at least commence litigation before you can meaningfully discuss settlement. Moreover, if one of the parties is disabled, the litigation process may need to be invoked for other reasons.

For the vast majority of separating spouses, however, litigation is just not necessary or productive. The clients who profit from litigation, who are able to endure the process and come out "better for it," are few and far between. For most spouses, lovers, and parents, the court process is a costly and horrific system that brings little happiness and leaves few survivors.

There's a story that is sometimes told about a wealthy and successful American entrepreneur. During an interview with a reporter, the entrepreneur is asked about his successes. He rambles on for several minutes about his properties, about various stock deals, land swaps, and several other clever accomplishments. He boasts about his cars, his corporate holdings, and his growing wealth. Then, the conversation turns to failures.

The reporter asks if the wealthy businessman has ever suffered losses.

"Oh yes," he reported, "I've had two very bad financial failures. Once, I lost a lawsuit. That cost me a king's ransom."

Then reporter asks, " … and the other time?"

" … was when I won a lawsuit."

There are many reasons to avoid litigation. Some of the most common reasons are financial. However, some of the best reasons for avoiding a lawsuit have nothing to do with money.

Civil litigation is a process that should be utilized for resolving disputes which cannot possibly be resolved by any other means.

In some matters, litigation is inevitable. For instance, if the truth is impossible to ascertain unless tested by a judge, a lawsuit may be unavoidable. In family law, however, the truth is rarely the main frustration. Most often, spouses know the truth and getting to the bottom of the story isn't the problem. Parties may occasionally lie or fudge the facts, but the truth is at least ascertainable, even if it's denied.

There may be a few exceptions to this generalization, of course. Sometimes, the facts are truly disputed. If one spouse believes, for instance, that the other spouse has been hiding assets (and it is denied), it might be necessary to test that hypothesis in front of a judge, where credibility can be determined. Usually, however, the "he said/ she said" contest in family law is largely immaterial, even though many litigants enrich their lawyers in the pursuit of winning such arguments.

In most family law cases, the facts are known with a high degree of certainty. That's because the two star witnesses in the case have "lived" the facts, and are intimately familiar with them. Even though they may disagree about what's best for the children, whether support should be paid, and who should get the home, there's often little argument over the facts.

As a result, litigation in family matters is rarely truly necessary.

What's surprising, however, is the number of family law cases where the parties approach litigation as (a) the best dispute resolution option, and (b) a practical method of resolving their dispute. In almost all families, better options exist. Moreover, litigation is usually anything but a practical method. Going to court to resolve matrimonial disputes is almost always expensive, unpleasant, cumbersome, and unnecessary.

In family law, almost all litigants lose. Even a wholly successful spouse, who claims to get everything, will typically later concede that the victory was illusory, unsatisfying, or Pyrrhic — achieved at excessive cost. Success in divorce litigation can bring some financial rewards, but it's rarely a pleasing process. I think this is because of what's at stake in family law litigation.

When couples who were once in love, raised children together, or shared aspirations, dreams, disappointments, and sleeping accommodations suddenly separate, discomfort is almost inevitable. Sometimes it's downright nasty. These feelings of loss tend to increase the stakes and make the transaction (the "business" of separation) seem more dramatic and traumatic than it needs to be.

It is normal to have differing views about what's right, how the spoils of the relationship should be divided, and what is best for children. Nuclear families argue about such matters all the time. When the parties are separating, it's to be expected that the dispute will appear to be more acrimonious and troubling. It is partly for that reason that non-acrimonious methods of resolving the dispute should be explored. Unfortunately, many separating spouses do not know what the options are, or why litigation is neither realistic nor affordable.

Some spouses can resolve their contests in a civil and friendly way, but they are the exception. Others must resort to dispute resolution systems such as arbitration, mediation, collaborative law, or the courts. Those who find a solution with minimal legal trauma are likely to be happiest.

The fact remains, however, that not all separating couples can sit down at the table and work things out. Sometimes, despite best intentions and sensible attitudes, settlement-minded spouses encounter difficulty. In fact, some of the most reasonable, wise, and balanced parents can lose all objectivity when it comes to divorce. Even good people may behave poorly during divorce.

Usually, when separating couples argue and go outside the relationship for help, they become involved in a process which was designed for general use by other people. In making these inquiries, the spouses may receive a referral to a mediator, counselor, or other expert. Maybe they'll start with a lawyer, their accountant, or their spiritual advisor. Whatever the case may be, spouses often look outside of their own family for advice and guidance when the topic of divorce comes up. Sometimes the advice that they receive is good, well intentioned, and helpful. Other times the advice is poor, incorrect, and potentially dangerous. Occasionally the advice is just plain bad, based on inaccurate information or ideas that aren't likely to be helpful. Getting really good and accurate information at the outset is very important.

Whenever spouses enter into mediation, arbitration, or the litigation process, some of the decision-making power is transferred, or downloaded, away from the couple to a person who is an outsider. In arbitration, the parties hand over the decision-making power to someone who is similar to a judge. The process itself may be more friendly, streamlined, and less costly than court, but it's really the same sort of system.

In mediation, the parties retain the decision-making power and control the process to a greater degree. Still, they are engaging in a time-limited and costly program. Even though mediation may be the least costly of several alternatives, it will often involve lawyers and other experts, including the mediator who will charge for the service.

In a court case, the litigants throw up their hands in a sense of helpless dismay and say: "Here, judge, you decide! We know you're a complete stranger and you really don't know anything about us, but we would like to entrust you to make a good decision about us and our kids."

In some cases, the litigants then proceed to offer up a one- to ten-day *Reader's Digest* condensed version of their lives and disputes before asking the judge for a ruling. It's all very artificial and, quite frankly, a little weird. It's also very costly.

I have been appearing before judges for 25 years. During that time, my office staff has dispensed more Kleenex than most funeral homes. We have also listened to more stories about relationships than most people can imagine ... and some of the stories we're told are incapable of being imagined by anyone. As we often say, the difference between truth and fiction is that good fiction must sound as though it could be true. That's not so with the truth. The stories told in our offices sound like they couldn't possibly be true, even though they are.

By far the greatest influence on my understanding has come from the several thousand divorces I have handled over the years. While it's overstating the obvious to say that each divorce case is unique, it may not be so obvious (though far more important) to note that in many respects, every case is the same.

Every separating spouse comes to me with a certain set of concerns. These concerns are universal. They arise independently of whether the relationship involves young or aged spouses, gay or straight parties, married or common-law couples, or any combination of the above.

Somehow, they all have the same kinds of problems. Familiarity with these themes and issues is something which allows me the opportunity to explain how separating spouses can resolve their disputes without a legal bloodbath.

It all really begins with one simple commitment — that separating spouses must make a good, solid, and honest effort to solve their matters outside of court. It's that simple. If you have that commitment, anything's possible. If you don't care and you're ready to go to court, good luck to you.

You may not have the commitment I speak of on the day you separate. Your world when the relationship ends is more likely filled with anger, disappointment, self-doubt, and other legitimate worries. About the last thing you want to do right after separation is offer commitment and accept your estranged spouse's professed commitment. There's no need to be reasonable — you're angry and hurt.

When you separate, you should settle your case without court (but probably with legal advice) in order to save money, save hardship, and avoid making a public display of your misery. Do it without court for all these and many more personal reasons.

Court is not a reasonable alternative. I say that in this book about 100 times, mostly because it's so important that I hope it will be remembered. And I say it knowing that those who work in the justice system (the courts) do their absolute best. I know as well that judges work hard and do their best with the information at hand.

Almost every time I appear in court, I'm impressed with the insight, intelligence, and clear thinking demonstrated by the judiciary. Time and time again, I hear persuasive and convincing arguments by skilled counsel, who offer up well-reasoned presentations for judges who are duty-bound to dispense justice. It's an awesome process indeed. If you ever doubt the integrity of this system, I urge you to sit through three complete trials. I warrant that your respect for the North American justice system will be indelibly affirmed in the process. Really, it's a remarkable system.

Having said all that, court can be a costly, slow, and awkward process. Judges do the best they can with the information they have, but it's no easy task. The court can apply the law to the known facts, but legally trained judges are not omniscient and they do not practice psychiatry. They are not counselors, and they are not permitted the luxury of sympathy. Judges are paid and duty-bound to decide cases and that's what they do. And almost every time a judge decides a case, somebody's unhappy. Sometimes, both parties are unhappy.

When litigants give over to a judge the power to decide their future, they enter into a process that's full of risk and uncertainty. Our justice system is not only harsh, traumatizing, and slow, it's also very costly. In Canada (where I practice), the cost of an average divorce trial is between $25,000 and $50,000. As I often tell my clients, "I've been a divorce lawyer for 25 years, and I couldn't afford me."

There are other costs to litigation as well. Telling strangers about your life, your secrets, your desires, and your worries is upsetting. When warring spouses download their personal information to a judge or an arbitrator, the opportunity for more hurt feelings is expanded and amplified. The chance to resolve the dispute in privacy and with dignity is gone. As a result, the litigation process itself may make matters worse. I see this sometimes in my practice. It's a situation that is played out with regular frequency. Imagine the following scenario:

The wife retains counsel because she's in need of spousal support. All she wants is some support (alimony) for a few years so she can get back on her feet. She's been out of the job market for a few years, and wants to retrain. Her lawyer must start a lawsuit to obtain that relief. He prepares affidavit material, explaining briefly the history of the marriage, and the career circumstances, and he describes the roles which the parties assumed during the relationship. He hopes to use these materials to persuade the court that the support is merited. As part of that process, it is explained that the wife ended her studies at university to raise the couple's only child. The lawyer thinks this may be important. The wife's affidavit also says that in recent years, she's longed to upgrade her skills and return to school, but never had the time or the opportunity. It's all pretty innocuous stuff. It is, however, necessary to deliver it to the husband and his lawyer to get the process started.

Although the allegations are not particularly provocative, the husband is upset by them. He worries that he's being persecuted, and wonders if the judge will tag him for some unmanageable monthly sum. As a result, the husband becomes defensive. He meets with his lawyer, and they prepare an affidavit in response. (This responsive material tends to be slightly inflammatory, based on the theory that a good offense is the best defense. The lawyer wants to have a fighting chance.) Accordingly, in the material, the husband says that the wife was always a little on the lazy side, and that's why her career never advanced. Really, it wasn't his fault — he wished she had worked more, and contributed to the family pot. He deposes that he often asked her to return to work, but she declined his sensible proposals.

The husband's affidavit goes on to refute the allegation that there was no time for school — and he points out that the wife always had time for secret romantic visits with the neighbor (partly because he feels that's relevant, and partly because he wants someone else to know what she did to him). It ends with his comment that he's exhausted and depressed as a result of her adultery, an allegation that may or may not be true, but is probably irrelevant in most jurisdictions. Anyway, the husband throws it in, saying that her infidelity has affected his ability to work overtime, and he says he's struggling at work. He needs time to take care of his personal issues, and is no longer willing or able to work overtime. This too has a financial cost.

She responds angrily. Initially, she felt that her allegations were all relevant and "sanitized," but her husband's comments have hurt. This time, she deposes that he was nasty throughout the relationship — his behavior drove her into the arms of the neighbor. She says that she resisted her husband's obsessive demand for her to perform meaningless fast food restaurant work because she knew that their ADHD child needed help with schoolwork and he was always unable to understand that. She uses unpleasant adjectives to describe his character flaws. She closes with a shot about how he's tired because he's overweight from beer consumption and watching sports on TV (something he did all day, every weekend) and that he's never been any good at getting available overtime.

Now the nastiness takes on a life of its own, and the course is set. The mother, who initially only wanted a little spousal support, is embroiled in a complex web that involves escalating legal expenses and revolving accusations. With each passing day she remembers something else that should be included in yet another affidavit, and she's on the phone with the lawyer twice a week. The husband cannot focus on work, and is considering stress leave. He starts to gather documents to prove what he says, and drops them off at his lawyer's office. There are more documents each week.

Soon, this little brush fire will spread. In a moment of extreme despair, the wife may even tell their daughter about the problems and Dad's allegations, and then, because she needs support for her position, she will involve the child in the dispute. The child *will want to support her mom, because all kids say what they believe their parent wants to hear. Accordingly, the daughter may say that she doesn't want to see her father, thinking this will please her mother. Soon, the father begins to fear parental alienation.*

Meanwhile, the father will attempt to garner sympathy by sharing information about the spousal infidelity. He'll tell his friends, and maybe the wife's sister (he's always liked her). The husband decides that if there's going to be a war, it will be necessary to hide some of the savings, and soon this brush fire becomes a raging inferno. The lawyers gobble up retainers at breakneck speed, and as the stakes increase, both litigants are beyond the point of no return very quickly. The equity they once had in their family home will be squandered on legal fees, transcripts, and document production. In the end, everyone loses.

At the end of this case, both spouses are miserable and broke of course. Their child is confused and unhappy. Had the parents settled, their daughter could have attended college. Instead, the lawyer's kids get a master's degree. Really, it's survival of the fittest in this melee.

What has occurred in this hypothetical example is a disaster which is played out regularly in law offices and courtrooms every day. It starts rather simply, with a short affidavit in support of a motion for one form of relief. Soon, the dispute expands, and the allegations grow like a life-threatening cancer.

The affidavits, which start the process off, are particularly toxic because of the procedure — they are "sworn" and usually "served" (delivered by a process server). And because the words of the affiant (a person making an affidavit) are sworn to as part of a Jurat (a certificate or place on the affidavit stating the time, place, and witnesses of affidavit) and given under oath, they are particularly stinging. Nothing hurts like the accusations of a spouse, sworn and shared.

Litigants know that the material is seen by at least several lawyers, secretaries, and court staff, and they may even believe (rightly or wrongly, depending on where the case is proceeding) that the lawsuit is a matter of public record, to which the world has access. Lawsuits, generally, are not secret.

In this example, the cost of the litigation grows exponentially with each new event. It's not unusual for the litigants to spend $10,000 in the first few months of litigation. That's before the matter actually reaches court for final determination. In fact, after all this hypothetical matter has gone back and forth, the prospects of settlement have become more distant than they were on the day of separation.

The spiraling costs of lawsuits are, however, but one reason for giving resolution without litigation a real and serious chance. Unspeakable accusations, affidavits that can't be withdrawn or forgotten, and allegations that contaminate parental relations are some of the other reasons.

Having said all that, I need to be cautious. No spouse should "turtle" on his or her basic rights just because of a fear of litigation. If you or your spouse face an unresolved legal issue, it *may* be necessary at some point to seek justice in the justice system. That system exists in our magnificent democratic society so that we can get help and justice when we need it. And, as I point out in Chapter 4, there are some specific circumstances in which litigation is the only option. In cases where one spouse has financial or psychological dominance, where abuse prevails, where children are at risk, or where assets have been hidden, a court case may be absolutely critical and the only route to peace.

In the vast majority of cases that I see, however, that's not so. I would estimate, in fact, that almost 90 percent of the cases where litigation has started are ultimately resolved outside of court. Many of the spouses who end up in litigation started in litigation, and they did so without finding out what alternatives existed. Many parties have not explored or exhausted the opportunities for a negotiated settlement when they consult counsel, and that is a mistake. Indeed, in most cases, it's never been tried. Often, that's because the parties simply don't know how to talk, how to negotiate, or what to do.

As you read the coming chapters, remember: The process of negotiation and settlement is something that your mediator or lawyer is going to engage in at any event — so why not at least try it yourself first?

If you're overweight, have high-blood pressure, and smoke cigarettes, you shouldn't be surprised when you go to the doctor for a check-up and receive advice about necessary changes. Unless you have absolutely no insight into the essentials of good health, you should be able to anticipate what will happen.

Yet when I see separated spouses and ask if they can really talk with their spouse or have a calm and meaningful discussion (in person or in writing), I often get a glazed look in response: "Can I do that? Can we talk?" is the question.

The answer, of course, is yes. Unless there's a restraining order that prohibits the parties from communicating, separated spouses *should* talk, provided it can be done respectfully and sensibly. If you can't do that, and every thought, proposal, and idea has to be delivered through counsel, you're going to need a patient lawyer and a large pile of money to resolve the issues.

At the start, I always tell my clients that the discussions have to begin somewhere. Try a simple issue that's not too emotionally charged and not likely to create great hardship. Establish rapport and build trust. Show your spouse that talking about the issues (in person, on the phone, or by email) doesn't need to be traumatic.

If you end up with a skilled mediator or lawyer, he or she will do the same thing. The mediator may not be able to resolve all the issues, but can probably find some common ground on some issues and capitalize on that. Small successes can lead to a trend.

You may want to start off with something that really is a nonissue. For instance, if you know that you have to pay child support and you know (roughly) what the amount will be, engage in a conversation about that. You may want to pretend that you need to discuss the topic because you want to talk about the format for the payments (whether it would be agreeable to split the payments in two, and pay half on the 1st and half on the 15th of each month). You do that knowing it's non-contentious, and hoping that the discussion will send a message that you intend to be fair. This kind of approach can help to create and build calm.

Even if you know that your spouse will never compromise on certain issues (custody, for instance), you may want to try to settle other issues such as money matters and leave the "unresolvable" custody issue for later. At the end of your discussions, you may be surprised to find that you have accidentally settled everything. Or perhaps you'll settle most of the issues and only need help on a couple of contentious points. If you eventually go to a mediator or lawyer with one issue instead of five, you're likely to be far more satisfied with the justice system, and you'll save a lot of money.

Before you do any of this, however, it's important to mentally prepare, which leads us to Chapter 3.

3

Think Positively about Your Divorce

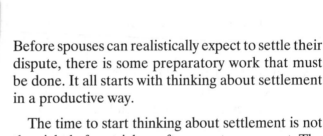

Before spouses can realistically expect to settle their dispute, there is some preparatory work that must be done. It all starts with thinking about settlement in a productive way.

The time to start thinking about settlement is not the night before trial, or after a nasty argument. The time for thinking settlement is now — at the outset — perhaps even before the physical separation has occurred. The sooner people realize that litigation is not a practical alternative, the sooner the focus can turn to productive, resolution-based thought processes.

I remember once, as a young man, hearing an environmentalist speak. It was in the late 1960s, long before it was popular to talk about pollution and litter and such matters. The speaker (I have forgotten his name) said that car manufacturers were treating the planet as though there was a spare tire in the trunk. That stuck with me.

By analogy, I would say that almost all separating spouses tend to approach the separation topics as though litigation is a spare tire. When they hear something they don't like, or when they encounter a settlement roadblock, they tend to posture by saying, "All right then, forget it. No more Mr. Nice Guy. Let's just go to court." It's an act of bravado and a demonstration of power. Those same spouses typically later report that the court process robbed them of their savings and ruined their lives. They also have horror stories about lawyers and how the case was mismanaged and so on. Unfortunately, they almost invariably forget that they made a deliberate decision to litigate.

Thinking about finding terms for a fair separation in a cooperative way is no small task. A separation or divorce proceeding usually signals the end of a relationship that was built on love, trust, respect, and romance. When those fundamentals are gone, it is sometimes hard to find peace or to negotiate anything. Bringing a previously loving relationship to an end is unlikely to create much happiness or anything positive. Happiness and divorce are concepts that really don't go together. Or do they?

When I die, I don't want anyone to gather around and mourn my passing, cry, or commiserate over what might have been. For one thing, nobody has ever been resurrected by such suffering. For another, there's simply no good purpose to be served by sadness. Instead, I want my survivors to have a party, to celebrate what good memories they may have of me, and to enjoy the camaraderie they'll share after I've gone. Maybe, in some way, I will have contributed to some of the good times in their lives. That will be my legacy, and that's what I hope will be celebrated after I'm gone.

When a loving relationship ends, there's similarly little value in crying over spilled milk. What's done is done. Keep the good memories that you have and move on. Avoid calling your separation a "failed marriage" or "disaster." Instead, try to think about the good times you had together, the fun you enjoyed as a couple, and then move on to other interests and, perhaps, other relationships. If that's impossible, it is still best to minimize the negativity and concentrate on what was learned and what lies ahead. If you approach the separation process this way, you may actually find the journey to be liberating.

In saying this, I am not suggesting that divorcing spouses should have a happy chat with their spouse, settle matters quickly, and then plan a big party to commemorate the end of ten years of misery. No one wants to gather up friends and family for a divorce fiesta. However, the fact is that divorce can and should be an event that signals the end of one chapter of life, and offers freedom and new opportunities for the beginning of a new and unwritten chapter. Whether the new experience begins at 29 or 79, it's an event that has *some* happy elements. Separating spouses who try to focus on the positive will likely find the process less trying.

I know this in part because of the hundreds of psychological reports I've read in custody cases. In my jurisdiction, when there's an apparently unfixable dispute over parenting, the parties or the court will often direct that a psychologist become involved. The idea here is that a psychologist will interview the parents and the children, and administer some tests. After that, the psychologist talks to the parties' collateral witnesses, and makes some observations and recommendations about the options for parenting. It's all set out in a big report, which usually costs many thousands of dollars.

In completing these tasks, the psychologist very often asks each parent a prearranged collection of questions. These questions are intended to elicit information about certain psychological issues in the family, and can provide helpful guidance to the expert. One question that's often asked is: "What are your spouse's best qualities or characteristics?" The answers given to this question are usually very telltale.

Spouses who are ready to move forward with optimism and productive energy will often frankly concede that their spouse has many good qualities. After all, some of these qualities must have been apparent at some point, or the parties would never have been together, and never would have formed a family and had children. Even though the parties are no longer in love when these questions are posed (and may, in fact, have many hotly contested, contentious topics to resolve), a "balanced" spouse will offer praise for a former lover's patience, wit, wisdom, cooking abilities, or other attributes. Even the smallest compliment is a good sign. A complete incapacity to remember any good traits is a very bad sign.

Those spouses who are unable to let go and instead derive pleasure from maligning their spouse will find it difficult to articulate praise. Any admission that the former spouse was good for anything is seen as a sign of weakness. The classic response from the "unbalanced" spouse will be that his or her former partner is devoid of any redeeming qualities. Sometimes the psychologist will simply say "in interview, Mrs. X was unable to recall any positive characteristics respecting Mr. X."

When I see this kind of comment, I know that the non-praising spouse has not prepared himself or herself for the process. There has been no commitment to the process, and I know that this spouse is unwilling or unable to embark on an intelligent, practical, or forward-looking approach to the issues and is likely still focused on blaming. Sometimes, this kind of unprepared spouse is having emotional challenges that will make him or her an easy target for the money-sucking litigation machine described earlier.

So what does this example tell us? It shows that having a positive and respectful attitude and approach isn't just a good preparatory tool — it's also good for your overall divorce health. Even though you are no longer in love with the spouse you've just parted from, you need to recognize that he or she has some good values and characteristics, even if you find that person frustrating, infuriating, and annoying.

Many years ago, I attended a wedding for a friend who had been previously married and divorced. The minister was a thoughtful and engaging speaker. During his address, he remarked that remarriage is a great endorsement and compliment to the institution of marriage. I found this refreshing, particularly from a religious leader.

Whether you accept this approach or not, the concept has merit. Despite all the reasons for despair during separation, it is to be remembered that the spousal relationship is worth preserving and pursuing again, even if your last relationship ended unhappily.

We see in everyday life that spousal relationships work well. Even though we know that not all relationships last forever, very rarely do we encounter warm, loving, rounded individuals who have never lived in a spousal relationship. Show me a person who's never known love, and I'll show you someone who is probably a fussy, selfish, miserly grump.

Having said that, our attitudes about the acceptability of divorce have changed. It's not improper now to mention that your spousal relationship is troubled, and it's not wrong to be divorced. There are exceptions, of course, but for most North Americans, being divorced just isn't a big deal. Our attitudes and the stigma of divorce have softened.

Interestingly, our willingness to divorce has been constant. Divorce rates have not changed significantly in the last four decades, and marriage rates have been surprisingly stable for many years.

Consistent divorce rates also tell us that unloved and unhappy spouses are not always willing to put up with bad relationships, and at least in North America, miserable spouses are saying that by getting divorced. Theoretically, at least, we are probably all contributing to a happier world by leaving unsatisfying relationships, and either living alone or finding functional spousal arrangements. In the long run, taking responsibility for your matrimonial health may be as important as taking care of your physical health.

Yet many unhappy spouses refuse to consider the divorce option. They take Herculean steps to avoid admitting that their marriage is not working. One of the best analogies used to describe this process goes like this: Having a bad marriage is like having a rock in your shoe. If you stay in the marriage despite the trouble, it's akin to learning how to walk with a rock that cuts into your skin with each step. The better approach, of course, is *not* to learn how to walk with the rock in your shoe, but to stop, remove the rock, and continue on without it.

Leaving a loveless marriage because you are able is better than remaining unloved. The old adage heard by many unhappy elders, "I stayed in the marriage for my children," is, with respect, nonsense. I suspect we knew this all along, but it was just too easy to stay on in a simple but loveless relationship. The by-product of those relationships, however, was a perpetuation of the problem. Parents who stayed in loveless marriages only managed to teach their children that it's okay to live in a loveless marriage. We should all want to show our children what a good relationship is like, and reinforce that an unhappy spousal bond is not good or normal.

In any event, this book isn't an exploration of the virtues of divorce. I am neither willing nor qualified to reassure separating spouses that they are doing the right thing. I'm not a counselor and I cannot debate the wisdom of separation or the cultural values of family law. There are many books available that are intended to help spouses improve or evaluate their relationship.

By the same token, this book isn't about the psychology of separation. Instead, the purpose of this book is to remind separating spouses of this: If you are really committed to resolving your family law issues in a calm, rational, fair, and sensible way, and if you really want to avoid hurtful and costly litigation, you need to get your mental health in order and approach the challenge with a positive and problem-solving attitude. If you do, your chances of success will increase exponentially.

If you have decided to separate, there are known techniques and advice about attitudes and approaches which can help to equip you with strategies allowing you to weather the storm. These techniques and advice can make the process of separation less painful. It all starts with a positive outlook. If you have that, and if you follow this advice, you may be able to separate with less pain, less expense, and less upset. To do that, you'll be negotiating your own resolution to your family dispute, and it will be on your terms — not terms imposed upon you by a judge or arbitrator.

1. Encouragement

Often, in my professional life as a divorce lawyer, I see people at their worst. When they come to my office, they are sad, distressed, angry, despondent, anxious, broke, or all of the above. Very often, they look exhausted, and behave poorly. Their judgment is impaired, and sometimes they are impaired: Many of my clients develop or increase their use of alcohol or other substances during the trauma of separation, and some go on to suffer chronic dependencies and worse. Very often, my clients tend to overeat or undereat. Some become exercise junkies, while others concentrate on doing nothing but consuming junk food, visiting casinos, or chasing new loves. Some put on a tough front and start dating right away (often before finishing the previous "business"), and some even buy houses and have children in new relationships before they are divorced — this I do *not* recommend. Occasionally, my clients go on buying sprees, dating sprees, travel sprees, or otherwise overindulge.

For most, divorce is a time of great personal psychological and social instability. All the safety nets have been removed and many feel quite empowered, while others feel powerless and vulnerable. Some are inexperienced on this emotional high wire, unsure of their next step, and need assistance to avoid a life-threatening fall.

Months or years later, I will see these people again. I bump into them when I'm shopping with my family, or I see them at the gas station, a sports event, or in some other nonprofessional context. Most often, this encounter occurs long after their case has been concluded, and their file closed. Often it's embarrassing for me because I am terrible with names. Most of my clients have only ever had one divorce lawyer, so it's relatively easy for them to remember my name. In my defense, I've had thousands of divorce clients, so recalling names is sometimes a challenge for me!

The point is this: When I see these former clients they look completely different. In almost every case where this has occurred, my former clients are only vaguely recognizable because they have changed — when I see them after the case is done, they are "normal." They are often outwardly happy. They are often in new relationships, or engaged in new ventures, careers, or activities. They are walking, talking, and carrying on the business of life. They are focused on things which are positive and they have reunited with the regular world. Their circumstances have changed, often in a positive way, and they are no longer dwelling on past hurts and the micromanagement of a legal case. They have moved on.

From this limited and anecdotal perspective, I know that if properly handled, a divorce can bring new happiness. Divorce is survivable, and it can be enriching. That does not mean that if you can resolve your divorce case, you won't have any other problems. No one can guard against other problems and challenges in life. That's simply impossible. But finding a resolve to an unhappy matrimonial situation can bring big relief.

So, in this book, I won't bother to persuade readers about the wisdom of the decision to divorce. Presumably, if you have bought this book, you've already made that decision. It's not my job to convince you that you're doing the right thing, or that you'll almost certainly be very happy afterward. No one can offer those guarantees. Besides, there are many excellent publications available to assist you in the process of personal recovery and rebuilding in the aftermath of divorce. Most are written by authors with psychological credentials which I do not possess.

Instead, this book is intended to make the separation and divorce process easier — survivable, and less unpleasant. In the process, it can help you find happiness at the end of a bad relationship. Get started now by reminding yourself that you are doing the right thing, and with the right attitude, you can resolve this issue. Get that rock out of your shoe!

2. Communication

In my firm, we find that many cases are easily settled when they receive early attention. The simplest cases to settle early are those where the parties are motivated and willing to listen. It helps, as well, if there's open disclosure.

Getting the discussion underway early is the key. In many cases, there is some sense of urgency (whether real or imagined), and so learning about perceived concerns before desperation sets in is critical. Sometimes, all that's needed is a single meeting and a few phone calls. Other times, a more intense course of discussions will be required. Either way, it all begins with communication. Doing the initial work to encourage good communication can save heartache and thousands of dollars.

Divorce case litigation statistics demonstrate that most cases (far more than half) will settle eventually. Most settle shortly before trial. In some jurisdictions, the overall settlement rate is close to 90 percent. What is acutely shameful about this statistic is that most of these cases settle in the last month before trial. That means that most — not *some*, but *most* — cases settle after the parties have spent several thousands of dollars on the process, and in so doing, created misery, unhappiness, and lasting memories about divorce. It's all a terrible waste.

I think this has some parallels to basketball. Despite the good work of Steve Nash, many Canadians don't know much about basketball. I'm a Canadian, and I know very little about the game. I do know, however, that on most of the occasions when I have watched basketball, I marveled at the scoring. To me, it seems obvious that the teams should each start with 80 points, and play for 15 minutes. No team ever seems to end up with less than 80 points, so what's the purpose? Playing a shorter game might not sell tickets or advertising, but it would take fans to the most important part of the game in an economical way.

The same sort of logic applies in respect to divorce litigation and settlement. Since we know that nine times out of ten a litigated case will eventually settle at the end, why not *start* with the settlement in mind, and only "argue" (or play) for 15 minutes? Since no sponsor is paying for advertising, and no fans are watching for a fee, there should be nothing wrong with focusing on the end game from the outset. Let's begin the process by talking settlement.

In fact, we should try to settle matters *before* the litigation begins. If we can do that, the parties can expect to save all kinds of heartache and expense associated with the litigation.

If this logic prevails and we start the discussions with settlement in mind, it should be much easier to settle before or without litigation, because the savings realized by not going to court will be available to "grease" the compromise. There will be more money available to make a deal before the court process begins because there are fewer expenses. The legal costs are minimal at the outset, and the trauma associated with running two separate households has not built any momentum.

So, early on, better settlement options exist. Each spouse can, in effect, afford to be more generous, because they know that if they do not settle at the outset, they will each spend more in the coming months. There is a significant financial incentive to settle at the start.

This point is often lost on newcomers to dispute. Very often, parties simply will not be able to understand that it becomes more difficult to settle after the litigation expenses have mounted.

This phenomenon is perhaps easier to explain in the context of a poker game.

When players at the poker table elect to play their hand or "stay in the game," they offer an ante. It's their commitment to the other players. They are sending the message that they think their cards are good, and they are willing to risk some money to prove it. This ante is their stake. It's money paid to carry on.

As the play moves around the table, and the other players join in, the stakes increase. By the time the next round of betting approaches, each player is being asked to increase the stake he or she is offering, and the ante rises.

It's like that in litigation too — as the process of negotiation or litigation continues, the cost of it all mounts, and the ante in the settlement game is increased. Sometimes, this is due to filing fees, experts' expenses, lawyers' bills, and other costs associated with processing the case.

At some point during a poker game, players may make salvage decisions, and determine that it's best to limit their inevitable losses by folding. At that point, they toss their cards, sacrifice their ante, but live to fight another day. Often, that's a wise move, particularly if the other players have better cards.

However, some ill-advised poker players come to a point in the betting process when their thinking changes — they actually start to believe that the stakes are so high they simply cannot afford to fold. Ancillary to that is the thought that their cards are not that bad, and in this time of changing perceptions, they begin to sense a kind of invincibility. In this thought process, the option of sacrifice is discarded. The thinking goes like this:

"I'm so far into this situation that if I quit now, I have nothing. I might as well go for it. If I fold, I will certainly have nothing, but if I gamble and go all in, I just might win. It's a long shot, I know, but it's the only chance I have. Besides, maybe this two of diamonds and seven of clubs hand isn't as bad as it looks."

This logic works well for the hero in a Bruce Willis action flick, but not so well for separating spouses.

Spouses in a separation dispute sometimes begin to think this way partway through the divorce case. They convince themselves to stick to their guns, in the mistaken belief that there are no alternatives. Still others play on, convinced that their crummy cards cannot be beaten.

Sober, experienced, and intelligent poker players know when to fold and cut their losses. They understand that surprise and disappointment can be visited on any player, and that some positions are simply too risky. They know that the likelihood of overall success can be increased by choosing to quit when circumstances warrant.

In divorce negotiations and litigation, these principles are often overlooked or totally forgotten. Separated spouses become positioned, certain that their views will be proven and accepted, and convinced that their chance to prevail will prevail. They begin to believe propositions that would never seem logical to an outsider (someone who has not lost objectivity in the process). Most often, these litigious believers are wrong.

When separating spouses become certain of their own invincibility, they become reckless with their money. Like drunken card players, they throw ever-increasing monies into the pot. They spend wildly on lawyers, accountants, experts, and processes, all in an attempt to demonstrate that what they want, believe, or expect is fair. Many times, they come to the point of no return early in the litigation, and then it's too late to back out. They are, in a sense, "all in." This happens frequently when litigation rages.

That sort of process almost never develops if there is no litigation, and if the parties negotiate matters outside of the court process. So keeping an eye on settlement options from the outset is wise. If separating spouses can start the process with concessions and compromise in their hearts, the chances of a happy and inexpensive resolution are increased. In so doing, the parties will maintain enough of the family wealth that perhaps they can do something smart with the spoils later — something that doesn't involve gambling!

3.   Why Can't Couples Settle Immediately after They Separate?

It's sometimes impossible for cases to settle early. Even though we know how important it is to try to settle early, it is often unmanageable, no matter what the effort or commitment. The question then becomes: Why can't spouses settle immediately after they separate? What happens over time to make settlement possible the night before trial, but not the month after separation?

I believe that there are several answers to these questions and several reasons why the cases which eventually settle do not settle early. Knowing these reasons should help separating spouses chart the course for their case in order to increase the likelihood of early settlement. Accordingly, we will examine these reasons in turn:

Reason number one: When parties first separate, they lack the knowledge about what lies ahead and do not understand their options. If they only knew something about the process, they would be inspired to talk, negotiate, and resolve their issues.

Solution: Get educated, and do it quickly. Since psychologists tell us that most separating parties do not reach the decision to part ways swiftly or without deliberation, it should, in fact, be entirely possible to get the information that's needed about separation before the actual separation. Getting some literature on separation and a free initial appointment with a family law lawyer is easy. Do it now, and learn what you need to know to make the correct decisions at the outset.

Reason number two: When parties first separate, they lack proper financial disclosure. They don't know enough about their assets, liabilities, taxes, or other matters (often financial), and are often overwhelmed by the scarcity of knowledge.

Solution: Get acquainted with your financial affairs before you separate. If you have never taken an interest in such matters, or for any other reason simply aren't aware, learn what you can as fast as you can.

Gather up your tax returns, bank statements, and other relevant materials and talk to an expert. A lawyer can be very helpful, or you may want to meet with an accountant. If those resources simply aren't available, consider retaining a chartered accountant (CA), certified management accountant (CMA), financial planner, or other expert to help you gather up the necessary information. Sometimes a friend can help. Talk to a retired banker, someone who has taught bookkeeping, and take advantage of whatever resources are available. While I do not recommend taking long-term financial planning advice from the local calculus instructor, there will be people in your area who are willing and able to help you gather the information you need to get started. Do that sooner rather than later. If the issues are significant, pay an expert accountant for advice.

The more you know, the better. Being informed and taking responsibility for your own financial welfare is as fundamental as the need to care for your own physical health. If you don't know what to do (for whatever reason), at least recognize that your ignorance is problematic and vow to find out. You'll have to learn sooner or later anyway. It's best to get on top of the issues now. You simply cannot spend the balance of your life not understanding the financial issues.

Reason number three: When parties first separate, there's uncertainty. Some may have thoughts of reconciliation. Others may be reluctant to admit their desire for separation, thinking that keeping the situation secret may be wise. After all, it's embarrassing to discuss a relationship that ended.

Solution: Get over it. If you are separated, or are seriously thinking about separation, you need to take these issues very seriously. If you reconcile later, you can easily stop the process and reconcile your situation with no harm done. Denying the existence of the problem, or worse still, pretending you don't have a problem, is like pretending you don't smoke while chatting with the oncologist. Remember that most people who die from choking do so alone — and most are alone because they ran off from a dinner table because they're embarrassed about choking. Any one of their guests might have saved them, but they choked alone in order to save face. It's like that in family law too. If you have family issues, those issues need to be dealt with. Having discord or unhappiness in a relationship is neither unusual nor anything to be ashamed of, so you need not worry about how you look in the eyes of others. What's important is that you recognize the significance of the changes that are occurring. If you face up to your concerns now, chances are you'll be better able to effect a speedy and trauma-free solution to those worries.

4. You Can Be Happy with Your Divorce

The basic theory here is that you can survive your separation or divorce process, and be happy after you reach settlement. The process need not be overly pricey, miserable, or challenging. This basic theory is built around the following concepts:

- **Most people do not want to fight.** Most separating spouses are leaving a relationship because they have had enough fighting, and want less fighting, not more. Knowing that, it should be possible to arrange the issues in a way that increases the prospects of settlement and gives the parties a way out of their strife. One way is to remind your warring spouse that once the settlement is done, there will be peace.

- **Most contested/acrimonious divorces are not necessary and can be avoided.** This is possible unless one or more of the parties is untruthful, psychologically unstable, or disabled. If you are exiting a relationship clouded by dishonesty, instability, mental illness, or disability, the concepts in this book may not be overtly helpful. For all others, you have nothing to lose by reading on.

- **It is entirely possible to calmly settle a divorce case.** Even if the relationship breakdown has been traumatic due to infidelity, emotional upset, or other personal disappointment, the process of separating need not be traumatic. In fact, if the split has been hard, you should commit to making the resolution easy. You deserve peace.

- **In this process, it is possible to engage accountants, lawyers, and counselors at a reasonable cost.** Not all expert help is expensive, and sometimes, not getting expert help is very pricey. I argue that experts must be brought into the process, on certain limited terms and for specific limited purposes. Properly managed, these resources can be accessed at a reasonable cost.

- **It won't take forever:** If you follow the concepts set out in this book, and keep these ideas in mind, you should be able to navigate your way through this treacherous channel and out into the open water that lies beyond divorce. It shouldn't take years. I can often do a separation agreement and process a divorce in a couple of months. Set your sights on that.

4

What You Need to Know about Hiring Legal Counsel

When you meet with a lawyer, tell the whole truth and nothing but the truth. Then, the lawyer can give you the advice you need and deserve. What you do with that advice is up to you.

A lawyer cannot help you unless you explain the story frankly. Withholding embarrassing facts, unsavory details, or shameful conduct won't help. When you talk to counsel, you are in search of advice, so candor in your reporting is an absolute necessity. If you don't tell the story frankly, you will obtain incomplete or inaccurate advice. Remember that the lawyer isn't being retained to be a friend — he or she is offering legal advice. The story you report, and the advice you get, is protected by privilege. That means that the meeting is confidential, and the lawyer cannot share it with anyone else without your consent.

Although I tell almost every prospective client all these things in our first meeting, I often do not get the whole story from clients. Some clients are ashamed of what they have done and said, so they try to give me a whitewashed version of the disputed events. Others think that it's none of my business, and so they'll only share certain facts that are absolutely necessary. The full truth inevitably surfaces, and when it does, there's trouble.

You need not worry about embarrassing yourself in the presence of the lawyer. Almost any experienced divorce lawyer will have heard stories far more outrageous, outlandish, and horrific than anything you can say. Even if your tale truly is new and surprising, so what? You are in the lawyer's office to get advice. Tell the story, and get the advice. If you don't, it's like going to the doctor's office with a sore throat and not mentioning the symptoms. The diagnosis is bound to be useless without the whole story.

We lawyers know that our clients are not visiting us because all is well. Most divorce lawyers deal exclusively with clients who are unhappy, sad, stressed, and pressured. We are trained to give advice in such circumstances.

Despite all that training and experience, lawyers generally have bad reputations. As a judge once said to me, "only about half of that reputation is earned and deserved." Still, the fact is that most lawyers (particularly family law lawyers) work long, hard hours in stressful conditions, and make modest incomes. Their work is often very unrewarding. Sometimes, family law lawyers work hard for clients who do not pay, and sometimes, when they do a particularly good job, they earn no praise or respect for it. You don't need to have sympathy for any family law lawyer, but it is wise to keep these concepts in mind when you meet with a lawyer.

In my career, I've acted for some fairly unsavory characters. I have represented men who don't want to pay child support, women who want to collect spousal support for improper reasons, and parents and spouses of all types and kinds who are driven by greed, hatred, and other improper motives. I have acted for these people because they are entitled to representation and because I hope and expect that I can make things better. Maybe I can persuade the man who's opposed to child support that his kids are deserving of help. Perhaps I can convince him that the fact that he must make a child support payment to his ex is a temporary situation that can change when his youngsters have grown into young adults and are able to handle money. Sometimes, I believe that I can motivate people to turn their lives around, find a new career or purpose in life, or understand that their present misery is transitional and that things will change. Occasionally, I act for spouses who have hidden assets and deliberately concealed income. With those clients, I act not to perpetuate the deception, but to bring reason and fairness to the process. I tell them that they must come clean, and I explain how that can be done. Sometimes, I must ultimately fire those clients and refuse to represent them. If they do not agree, I cannot perpetuate a lie.

At all times, I owe a duty to the court to not promote a fraud or deceit. Like all lawyers, I must represent my clients with integrity, energy, and commitment, but I won't lie for them, and I won't permit them to mislead the court. It's not often an easy job. It is, however, a helping profession that's exciting and filled with challenges. The challenges and stresses are what make the career exciting.

Most lawyers you meet (particularly if you are meeting family law lawyers in regard to your divorce) will *want* to help you. They will be genuinely interested in your story, your problems, and telling you about the possible outcomes and solutions. I've been doing this job for many years, and I can tell you unequivocally that I still look forward to every new consultation. Most often, the story that's told is fascinating. And, at the end of it all, I get an opportunity to offer advice and my opinion about what can be done to fix things.

When you contemplate divorce or separation, you should avail yourself of the desire which most family law lawyers possess — to listen and help. Getting information and advice about your separation need not be difficult or costly. Almost all family law lawyers love to talk, and most offer free initial consultations. Most will give *some* advice for free. You may want to ask yourself if dentists, taxi drivers, or mechanics offer this free service.

In my practice, I sometimes find my clients insisting I take unnecessary steps, or initiate actions which are unlikely to produce an appreciable legal result. Occasionally, I actually argue with my own clients about what should and should not be done on the case. It's not a very flattering or productive exercise, but from time to time it is necessary. If I took all my instructions and followed through on every step that clients asked me to take, I'd be considerably more wealthy, but I would have a poor reputation in my professional community.

If you do hire a lawyer, take the lawyer's advice. If he or she cautions against a certain step, position, proceeding, or course of action, listen. Do not march off on your own agenda. If you feel that you are not connecting with your lawyer and that your issues are not being understood or addressed, speak up. If you're still not happy, get a second opinion.

Clients often do not understand this. They may confuse a lawyer's advice or insistence with personal resistance. For instance, I sometimes encounter a client who is unwilling to pay child support because the custodial spouse is in a new relationship. Almost invariably, that has nothing to do with the obligation to pay child support and I say so. Occasionally, this angers my clients, and they mistakenly assume that I don't care about them, or that I am unwilling to follow their instructions. At that point, it's time for me to explain.

If you are dealing with a lawyer and you have the sense that your wishes are not being heard or respected, say so. Make it your job to find out why there's resistance.

Remember that there are some lawyers who, properly retained, will do almost anything that the client instructs, even if it's unwise, impractical, or unlikely to produce an appreciable result. Sometimes, a needy client can take strength from a compliant lawyer who will write demanding letters and make various threats about litigation and other steps that will follow if such and such is not done. This behavior is destined to quickly extinguish the retainer, and bring little happiness to your life.

1. When Should You Hire a Lawyer?

When you separate, you will probably need a lawyer at some point during the process. In my view, there are several key times described in the following sections when you should consult counsel.

1.1 Before you separate

When you plan to separate, see a lawyer for a free consultation. Do that *before* you move out or separate. Plan to spend 30 to 60 minutes with a lawyer to discuss your options before you leave. Getting some initial advice about your options, the process, and your vulnerabilities will be helpful. You may find that it's not wise to leave the home. You may learn that you should take your car and personal belongings, but little else. If you move out without canvassing your options and issues in advance, you may be in for a surprise. The advice you receive will depend on your circumstances, situation, and jurisdiction.

Most family law lawyers will be willing to discuss your situation frankly with you, often for free, in an initial consultation. If you absolutely cannot obtain a helpful initial consultation for free, pay for an hour of time. It's money well spent. Try to talk to a senior, experienced divorce lawyer.

Go to the appointment with specific questions in mind. It's best to write down your questions before the meeting so that you are not confused or distracted. Do not try to record the answers (you'll probably remember 99 percent of what you hear anyway), as that can offend some counsel. You should, however, try to use the time wisely. If, after your meeting, you are still unsure about what to do, book a second consultation. You will probably be expected to pay for that second visit, but it will be worth the investment.

1.2 Before you sign any documents

Always talk to a lawyer before you sign anything, even if the document seems relatively harmless. That advice extends to leases, mortgages, transfers, loans, guarantees, and any other legal document with legal consequences.

Every week I meet people who have, without any advice or information, signed mortgages, lines of credit agreements, house transfers, guarantees, and other corporate and personal documents of great significance. Trying to undo these documents later is often a considerable and costly challenge. In fact, I reckon that about one third of my annual income is earned trying to get clients out of bad deals they have made. So if you are ever faced with an invitation to set your name to anything which remotely resembles a legal document, get advice *before* you sign. This advice is acutely important if you are facing a separation or divorce, or if your spouse is likewise inclined.

1.3 If something doesn't feel right

Talk to a lawyer whenever you feel overwhelmed, overpowered, uninformed, or uneasy with the separation process. If the negotiations or discussions don't feel right or sound right, talk to counsel. More often than not, your senses will be right. If you feel as though you're in over your head, you probably are.

2. How to Find a Lawyer

Getting legal advice freely or cheaply is an opportunity that should be utilized. In my firm, we offer a free initial consultation (usually 30 to 60 minutes) and will sometimes even offer a second interview or telephone conference before turning on the meter. We do it with no expectation of gain because we like to help, and frankly, it's sometimes better and less expensive to answer a question on the phone or in an interview than to open a file and incur costs that may not be recoverable. We take no pleasure in leading clients in unwanted directions, and we have no desire to make trouble where no trouble exists. Furthermore, if some or all of the issues can be resolved without a lawyer, we'll say that. Most lawyers offer similar advice.

I tell new consultations about their options and the opportunities for self-help resolution. If they have a simple problem, or an issue that can be resolved without great expense or legal expertise, I say so. There's no point in my doing work for someone who doesn't need it. People respect that. If they have an involved or complicated question, we know that they will probably hire us, and they do return when they truly need us.

You can start the process by calling a few local lawyers that you found on the Internet or in the Yellow Pages. If the lawyers won't see you for a free consultation, keep calling. In all but the most remote locations, inexpensive or free interim legal advice should be available.

If it isn't, and if the lawyer you want to see is willing to meet, but only if a fee is paid, ask for additional information. How much is the fee? If you decide to retain the lawyer, is the fee applied against the ultimate account? If the lawyer wants $100 for a half hour of advice (and that advice can set your mind at ease or save you $500 later) that's $100 you cannot afford to save. Don't be a pain in the neck on the initial call, but do ask probing questions which you need to have answered. You can probably obtain most of the basic information about the initial consultation and its cost on the phone with the secretary.

Try to avoid making decisions about hiring a lawyer solely on the language on the Internet, or the strength of his or her advertising. Some of the most effective lawyers I work with do not advertise at all. Some of the biggest and boldest advertisers are the weakest counsel. You may want to start your search on the Internet, but use other resources, and your gut reaction, as well.

Ask for referrals from friends and family, but make the ultimate choice based on your instincts and research, not what others recommend.

Some lawyers will see you for a consultation and give you their thoughts in an informal way. Others won't be interested in doing anything unless they have been retained. Sometimes, that means they want money up front, or they are too busy or uninterested.

If the lawyer you want to see won't talk to you without a cash deposit, consider carefully whether you want a trust-based relationship with that professional. You may conclude that you deserve to at least meet the lawyer and have a chat before you spend money or lock yourself into an important contract. Personally, I would steer clear of any family lawyer who won't see you once for free or for a modest fee.

When it comes to finding a good lawyer, there's much to say. In no particular order, here are my thoughts about how to select a lawyer:

- Make finding competent counsel your number one priority, and spend some time and energy on that. When you really need a lawyer, forget the horror stories, lawyer jokes, and advertising slogans.

- Interview several lawyers. The "right" lawyer for your friend might not be the "right" lawyer for you. Shop around, and be critical. You need not share your impressions with the lawyer during the interview (after all, it's not a talent show), but you should make some point-form notes to refresh your memory later.

- Remember that because most lawyers offer free initial consultations, you have nothing to lose by seeing two or three before you decide. After all, it's an important choice you're making. Try to spend at least as much time choosing your lawyer as you did choosing your car.

- Know that there is no "best" lawyer just as there is no best goalie, car, or quarterback.

- Explain the basic facts during the interview, and then listen carefully to the advice. Don't try to get a complete resolution in the first half hour; instead, listen to the questions and answers and ask yourself if you are getting a sensitive, thoughtful explanation, or a rehearsed one-size-fits-all answer.

- Trust your instincts. Your choice of counsel is likely to be important, and it's hard and costly to change lawyers later.

- Take your time. Unless your case is a real emergency, plan to spend a little time interviewing lawyers and thinking about the options. It is far easier to spend two days selecting counsel at the outset than it is to change lawyers partway through your case.

- Do not hire a lawyer because he or she is tall, handsome, pretty, well dressed, or nice. Do not hire someone based on perceived reputation. Hire someone who seems like a fit to you, with your case. That lawyer should be someone you trust, and who seems to care.

- Do not hire a lawyer with whom you cannot communicate, or who frightens you. A bully who is a brute to your spouse may be equally difficult with you (the client), so watch out for that.

- Do not hire a lawyer because his or her office is nearby. Law is not convenient, and besides, in this electronic age, proximity is probably not a big deal.

- When you meet with prospective lawyers, ask them for other referrals. Experienced and confident lawyers know like-minded colleagues, and they will not be afraid to name the competition. In family law, there's generally plenty of work, so a good lawyer will probably be glad to offer comparables.

- When you have your free initial consultation, remember that the lawyer is not your friend, counselor, psychologist, or accountant. Ask for advice on legal topics within that person's area of expertise.

- Do not expect the lawyer to solve all your problems in the first consultation. It took years for your problems to develop and chances are that an instant fix is not at hand. In any event, the purpose of your meeting is otherwise. You are there to gather an impression of the lawyer and learn about his or her credentials, charges, and general manner. Decide what to do after the interview is done.

- Do ask about money. It's important to understand hourly rates, the disbursements policy, and estimates. Be frank, and don't pretend you understand if you don't.

- Once you have made your decision and decided who to hire, plan to pay. The quality of service you receive is likely indirectly connected to the proximity and promptness of your payment of accounts.

- Once you have hired counsel, follow the advice you receive. Don't hire counsel and then take advice from your hairdresser!

If you find that you do actually need a lawyer (and my view is that you will probably need a lawyer at some point, for some part of the process), get one. Hire a good lawyer.

Remember that the lawyer's professed reputation simply does not matter. Sometimes the best lawyers are new, young, unknown, or just starting out. Sometimes the old-timers are costly and careless. Sometimes the reverse is true. There are no rules about who's good. Take care with your decision. A bad lawyer is like a bad eye surgeon.

2.1 Prepare for the initial interview

When you go to the interview, take some notes. Jot down two to five questions you really want answered before you attend. Try to listen carefully. If you don't understand something that's said, ask for clarification.

At the interview, be prepared to tell your story in point form. Practice in advance, so that you can say it in ten minutes or less. Don't go into great detail about the marriage, or the reasons for the breakdown. Most of that is irrelevant anyway. You should be able to explain the basics. Be familiar with and able to list your main assets. You should be able to describe your liabilities too. Tell the lawyers about your spouse and his or her job and income, and list the kids, your job, your income, and so forth.

Next, try to create a concise list of the things you want to know. Try to prioritize, since there probably won't be time to talk about everything. If custody of the kids is a key issue, plan to talk about that. Explain why you think your spouse is not a competent caregiver, and be prepared to describe your idea of a sensible resolution to the issue. Get the lawyer's thoughts on the prospects of success, and listen to the advice you get.

You will also want to ask about the lawyer's skill, experience, and approach. Ask him or her how long he or she has been in practice, and inquire about support staff. Ask how the lawyer charges (hourly, lump sum, or some other method, and find out how much is required as a retainer). Ask if you can communicate by email.

3. Retainers and Legal Fees

A retainer is a deposit paid to the lawyer at the outset of the case, as a kind of down payment toward the future payment of fees and expenses. Most matrimonial lawyers will require a retainer before they perform any substantive work. Some will ask for a modest amount (e.g., $500 or $1,000), while others will require a significant retainer (e.g., $5,000 or $10,000, or even more). The retainer is occasionally negotiable, but many lawyers won't start work until they receive it.

The problem here, of course, is that most separating spouses are enduring financial struggles. That's typically so because when they separate, they are suddenly running two households on the same income that previously supported one. Separation is often a tough time, and many couples do not have extra cash lying around the house for lawyers.

From the lawyer's perspective, the need for a retainer is beyond doubt. Since the provision of legal services involves delivery of an information commodity, there is no "security" for the service, and no way to ensure or guarantee payment without money up front. A separating spouse can use the lawyer, take the advice and the benefit of representation, and walk away without paying. Many do precisely that. True, the lawyer can sue for fees, but that's not a productive use of the lawyer's time, and it's not the kind of relationship that should prevail between a lawyer and client.

If and when you retain a lawyer, there are several kinds of products and services that you may be charged for. The first and foremost is legal fees. That's the part of the bill that pertains to professional service and advice provided by the lawyer in the defense or prosecution of your case.

Most lawyers charge by the hour, but some charge based on the work done (task-based fees). Still others charge based on an advance estimate or *flat fee*, which is established at the outset. In matrimonial cases, it's almost always impossible to estimate what the case will cost at the outset, so very few family law lawyers operate on a flat-fee basis. However, there are a few exceptions:

- In my jurisdiction, I can almost always estimate the cost for an uncontested (or unchallenged) divorce. If there are no children and few assets, I usually estimate the fees at $1,000. Disbursements and taxes are in addition. If there are several kids, some assets, and a few other "tricky bits" to deal with, I may quote the fees at $1,500, but rarely is my professional charge any higher than that.

- Outside of family law, there are many legal services that are charged on a flat-fee basis which is almost always quoted or estimated in advance. One example would be a will. In most locations in North America, lawyers charge between $100 and $1,000 for a relatively simple or standard-form will. Another example would be the purchase of a family home (often with a mortgage or line of credit security agreement). Simple realty transactions are almost always completely predictable in price, and can be quoted at the outset.

• Specific task-based work where there is little legal skill involved, and a great deal of similarity from one client assignment to the next. Criminal pardons, simple immigration forms, notarizations, and independent legal advice are some examples.

Sadly, in family law, it's almost impossible to estimate fees in advance. However, you can ask for monthly bills or estimates so that you keep expenses in line.

When you hire a family law lawyer, legal fees are not the only service or product you'll pay for. In addition to the legal fees, there will be disbursements, charges for paralegals and support staff, and in many jurisdictions, taxes. Sometimes these can be very significant.

Disbursements are out-of-pocket expenses that the lawyer will pay while working for you. The most expensive of these charges will likely be for expert reports and the opinions of doctors, accountants, and others with specialized skill or knowledge. How and when do these charges arise?

Consider, for instance, a case where one spouse alleges a physical or mental disability that gives rise to a need for spousal support. In order to prove that the impairment disqualifies the spouse from paid employment, the lawyer will need expert evidence. Rarely will the court be satisfied with the lawyer's "say-so" and the client's own testimony about what he or she cannot do. Instead, the judge will want to hear evidence from a doctor who is qualified and competent to offer expert opinion evidence about the disability, the limitations on employment, the future prognosis, and other relevant matters. In some cases, it may even be necessary to arrange for vocational testing or an occupational assessment by a vocational expert, psychiatrist, or rehabilitation witness.

The same is true in a case where a lawyer needs to prove the value of a business, a significant asset (i.e., home, pension, or expensive vehicle), or any other item or matter which is beyond the ordinary knowledge of the average person. In short, if an expert opinion may be needed to prove any fact in a lawsuit, the lawyer will probably have to hire an expert who can investigate, review the facts, give the opinion in a report, and (if need be) testify in court.

These experts do not work for free. Some are more costly than others. For instance, in my area, I can probably find a property appraiser who will give an expert opinion about the value of a residential premise and testify in court for $1,000 to $3,000. However, if I need a psychiatrist to explain that my client cannot work due to depression, I can expect to spend $5,000, $10,000, or more.

Before your lawyer hires an expert and pays out large amounts of money, however, he or she will almost certainly forewarn you of the impending costs and seek your approval. It would be unusual for a lawyer to hire a pricey expert without explaining it to you, telling you about the costs, and seeking your consent.

Disbursements for less shocking costs will also be seen on your account. For instance, the lawyer may post disbursements charges to your account for postage, scanning, couriers, and court filing fees. Photocopying, binding, agents' fees, court reporters, interpreters, and other litigation expenses are also common expenses. These are the legitimate costs of doing business, and most lawyers are careful about recording such costs with care. You should, however, ask the lawyer in advance of the engagement about his or her practice and policy on such matters. If in doubt, ask.

Most lawyers are aware that clients — particularly family law clients — do not have endless supplies of money for lawsuits, and so they will try to keep costs to a minimum. It's good business to be unwilling to spend, and it just happens to be part of the ethical duty that lawyers owe to their clients and their governing law societies or bar associations. In any event, it's important to remember that when you get a bill for, say, $6,000 in a divorce case, less than half of the amount due may relate to the lawyer's fees. The balance can be made up of disbursements and taxes — all of which are a necessary part of the case, and all are payable.

Although it is sometimes alleged that divorce lawyers profit by causing trouble, it is an unlikely proposition. In the modern legal world, any lawyer who tries to make work by causing trouble would have a rotten reputation quite quickly and a professional citation to answer. The idea that lawyers cause litigation in order to earn huge fees is probably nothing more than an aged myth — and one that may never have been true.

I estimate that for about the last 30 or so years, almost every family law lawyer in North America has probably had more work than he or she can realistically complete. As a result, there's just no point in causing controversy to make work. Quite apart from ethics and morals, it just isn't necessary.

Remember, too, that lawyers are acutely aware that when a family breaks up, the financial pressures within the households are often exquisitely strained. They know that the window of opportunity for negotiating a good settlement will begin to close after the first few legal bills are paid. Counsel will focus on early resolution. Indeed, good lawyers will use the threat of ongoing litigation and the attendant costs of the court process as an inducement to compromise. It's a powerful motivator.

So, in summary, if and when you need a lawyer, you must plan ahead. Don't pass up the opportunity for legal advice just because you have heard horror stories about runaway legal accounts. Most lawyers will offer free initial consultations. If you need professional advice after, ask the lawyer about fees and charges, and try to pay as you go. If you are ever in doubt about what you're paying for, how the lawyer charges, or how much you have spent, get on the phone or email the lawyer and ask.

If you have decided to hire a lawyer, you will probably be asked to sign a retainer agreement. That document is a legal contract between you and the lawyer, and it explains the roles that you will assume in the relationship. The contract will say what work the lawyer will do, how he or she will charge for that work, and it will describe your obligation to pay. It may be a few paragraphs or a few pages, but either way, it's worth reading. If there is any part of the retainer agreement that is unclear, ask for an explanation. Don't sign it until you understand it.

One thing to watch for in the retainer agreement is the clause about "associates, paralegals, and secretaries." Almost every modern retainer agreement has such a clause, and it's worth a careful review. It is intended to explain the role that support staff will take, and if and when you'll have to pay.

Most experienced family law lawyers have support staff. Busy divorce lawyers may have several support staff. These personnel work with and for the lawyer, and some of them post their time directly to your account, while others work for and are paid by the office as an overhead or administrative expense. Associates (usually junior lawyers) and articled students (law degree graduates in the process of being licensed) may work on your file as well, usually under the supervision of the lawyer you hired. Understand how these personnel charge and what their costs are.

In almost all firms, senior, experienced lawyers are very busy, and they may not have time for every routine step along the way. Moreover, if cost is an issue, you don't need a senior litigator doing research work or drafting briefs and letters on your case. Lawyers know this, and utilize less costly staff whenever it's appropriate. This will help to lessen the cost to the client, and to ensure the orderly progress of the case. It may mean that the lawyer isn't working on your case every minute of every day, and that some of the less challenging tasks will be left to staff or juniors.

I find that some clients are suspicious of this. They wonder if they have been handed off to the junior person because I'm too busy. Whenever that complaint arises, I realize that the misunderstanding is my fault. I am responsible because I haven't properly explained how the office works.

Although not all law offices operate the way I do, it's my practice to delegate when I can. Giving routine tasks and less consequential aspects of the case to experienced staff can be very economical. My legal assistant, for instance, has 24 years of experience, is wonderfully talented, supremely even tempered, and wise about family law issues. Her input on most files is valuable and helpful, and it comes at about one-third of my hourly rate. The assistance she brings to clients is enormous, and it's all done at a fraction of my rate. There's good value there. Besides, she's pleasant, understanding, and usually in the office when I'm in court. My clients are wise to maintain a good professional relationship with my staff.

Still, if you are working with a lawyer who is never around, passes you off to the junior at every opportunity, and can't return a call, speak up. Most lawyers want to know if the client is dissatisfied, and are quite eager to problem-solve, provided your concern has some merit. If you don't speak up, the lawyer will probably assume that you're okay with what's going on.

At this point, a word of caution is in order. As you work your way through a legal problem and seek counsel and guidance from a lawyer, try to avoid being a problem client. Use your time with your lawyer wisely and stay on top of your account, but do not harass your lawyer.

A problem client is a client who needs attention every day or every week, calls regularly, complains often, and strains office resources nearly to the breaking point. Then, when it comes time to pay for the attention that has been demanded, there's trouble with the account.

If you are hiring a lawyer to help with your case (and, hopefully, to help you get it resolved without court), don't be a problem client. If you have pressing, urgent issues that need regular attention, say so, and then give the lawyer a chance to do the work. Of course, expect to pay when that work is done.

Almost all family law lawyers find it difficult or impossible to provide an advance estimate of the fees that will be incurred and charged. Senior counsel, with years of experience, will sometimes agree to provide a range of estimated costs and disbursements, but even that's tricky.

This problem arises not because lawyers choose to be deliberately vague about their fees. Indeed, most lawyers would prefer to be able to provide a binding quotation in advance of performing the work.

The trouble is that the expenses associated with a case are almost always impossible to estimate at the outset because each case is so very different. What a case costs is more often influenced by the personalities than the issues. A nasty and costly bit of litigation is almost always fueled by positioned, opinionated, and stubborn litigants. Very infrequently is the legal issue itself the cause of the expense.

Some of the most costly cases I've been involved with have been very simple matters from a legal perspective. These are cases where the facts are not particularly tricky, and the law is surprisingly simple. These big-fee cases are not typically about foreign assets, secret corporations, or hidden savings. In fact, the most expensive cases to litigate are usually those about custody of children.

Custody and access issues can be the most hard-fought and antagonistic battles of all. Parents, convinced that they are right and the other spouse is wrong, dangerous, meddling, alienating, or otherwise destructive, will hire lawyers, psychologists, experts, and litigate with a ferocity that really should be seen only at a boxing match. These disputes are almost invariably financially and emotionally crippling. Sometimes they are inevitable, but usually they are conducted by litigants in spite of the warnings of counsel. If you resign yourself to this kind of litigation issue, make sure that you are well positioned for the expense.

Your legal account, no matter how big, should always be a concern. Unless you are incredibly wealthy, legal fees are an expense that should never form part of a regular family budget. In order to ensure that it does not get out of control on you, ask your lawyer to send an updated bill every month. This will allow you to monitor your account regularly.

Make it your job to stay informed as your case progresses. If your lawyer does not normally produce regular accounts for you, it makes good sense to call regularly about your account, and find out exactly what costs and disbursements have been mounting. Don't be shy! Even if you don't want to pay your account weekly or monthly, you should stay informed at all times.

Also note that some lawyers may be willing to work for you on a piecemeal basis. This practice, sometimes known as *unbundling*, can work well in some circumstances. For instance, unbundled or task-based retainers are particularly useful where the need for service is limited to a particular project, such as a separation agreement. If you and your spouse have settled your differences, and simply want a lawyer to draft the agreement (i.e., to put it in writing) you may be able to obtain a firm quote or price for that work, and have that, and only that, done. Another example would be where you and your spouse have resolved matters and only want to engage a lawyer to prosecute the divorce. That too can sometimes be a simple task-based assignment that can be done for a set fee.

Yet another example would be a simple one-time meeting with a lawyer which is convened expressly for the purpose of obtaining independent legal advice (sometimes simply called ILA) about the fairness or propriety of a contract or agreement. Sometimes, clients simply want an hour with a lawyer to review an agreement, and ask for ILA for that purpose. Normally, the costs for that service range between $100 and $500, depending on what's involved. Remember, too, that there exists an odd relationship between a lawyer's perceived reputation, and legal fees. Sometimes, loud and well-known lawyers are the most expensive, though they may not be the best.

I remember once meeting a new client who was quite savvy about the legal profession. Every time an issue arose, he seemed to know about it, and whenever the conversation turned to lawyers, he knew several.

After a time, I asked him how he knew so much about the business of law. He explained that as a young man, he had once been charged with robbery, and from then on, he had taken an interest in all legal matters.

"I got off that charge, you know," he said, "but then again, I had John Doe the lawyer ... " There was a pause.

My client looked at me. "John Doe, you know, the famous criminal lawyer? Surely you must know him?"

I told him that I did know the "famous" lawyer. I had studied under him as a young lawyer.

"Well," said the client, "then you must also know he's the best!"

I did not want to confess that I was not privy to this obvious accreditation, but I was even more curious how the client knew that. So I asked, "How do you know that he's the best?"

The client answered promptly and certainly, "He told me so!"

4.   If There's Fear or Violence in the Relationship

Throughout this book, I encourage readers to consult with counsel from time to time as needed and I insist that a consultation occur before any important document or paperwork is signed. There is, as well, another occasion when counsel should be consulted.

If there is violence or oppression present in your relationship, you should obtain counsel. You should do it swiftly. In a relationship where there is fear, the early actions you take and the choices you make may significantly increase or decrease the likelihood of satisfactory resolution. Even if there's "only a little pushing and shoving" (as my clients sometimes say), there's a heightened need for professional advice and information. Do not fail to get that advice.

That advice stands, as well, in relationships where there is deception or oppression.

The reason for that advice is quite simple. This book, and the advice contained in it, is predicated upon a relative equality in bargaining power and the presumption that the parties are free to make their own decisions. If there's violence or abuse of any kind, that freedom is compromised, and you need to talk with professionals. In such circumstances, it is unlikely that you will be able to broker a fair solution on your own. Any deal, concession, or compromise that's made out of fear is almost certain to be inadequate and dissatisfying in the long term.

In spousal relationships that are based on inequality or oppression, there is sometimes a temptation to settle just to be free. Deals made in such circumstances typically bring neither peace nor freedom. Don't try to broker a deal simply to avoid further trouble.

I normally have about 100 divorce cases going at any given time and chances are that between 5 and 15 of these involve litigation instituted in an attempt to invalidate a bad bargain. Many of these bad deals have been made by spouses who have compromised unfairly because of fear, they were in a rush, didn't understand the issues, or felt pressured. Some of these clients are afraid of the process, some are afraid of the uncertainty, and many are afraid of their spouse. As stated, if fear or violence permeates your relationship, do not let it permeate your settlement process.

Remember, too, that most family law lawyers are experienced in handling cases where there is violence, fear, oppression, or other abuse (i.e., physical, psychological, or sexual). Sometimes, but not always, it is necessary to involve the police.

Some spouses are unable to recognize real danger. Perhaps that's because they have been in danger for so long that they do not recognize real risk when they see it. They have become insensitive to oppression and the fear of violence. Whatever the case, if oppressive behavior is one of the reasons for your separation, you will very likely need professional help — either from a lawyer or from the police or both.

However, some parties are hypersensitive to risk, and may even call the police as they near separation because they think it will help their case. To be sure that you are not overreacting or underreacting to fear, danger, and oppression, consult with counsel early on and take the advice that's offered. Most lawyers are keenly sensitive and well trained on these topics, and can offer invaluable advice about what to do.

5. Don't Make Any Decisions in Haste — Consult with Legal Counsel First

I believe that some bad deals are also made for the following reasons:

- *Impatience:* Sometimes, spouses are anxious to settle on a deal (any deal) and move on. This occurs, occasionally, because one spouse has become involved in a new relationship. Sometimes one of the parties is moving residences, changing lifestyles, or otherwise moving on. For spouses with this kind of agenda, making a hasty deal — and one that is unfair or improper — seems like a good idea. Separating spouses who are impatient are often vulnerable to improvident bargains.

- *Anger:* Do not give your lawyer instructions to do anything when you are angry. Some attorneys enjoy bargaining with an unrepresented and impatient spouse because they recognize that they can make a very advantageous deal with a spouse who's in a rush. For what it's worth, if you make a bargain when you're in a hurry, and because you're in a hurry, you are probably making a bad deal. I liken haste in the process to throwing out an entire wardrobe after the loss of five pounds on a fad diet. In the long run, it's behavior that you're likely going to regret.

- *Separation:* A desire to add formality to the separation, and finalize the end in a comprehensive way. Some spouses want to make a deal quickly because they want to know that they are done. They may have a little self-doubt, some insecurity or uncertainty about their past decisions, and they feel that a separation agreement and/or divorce will insulate them from that.

- *Guilt:* Sometimes one or both spouses feel guilty about ending the relationship. That can be because they feel as though the demise of the relationship is blameworthy. Maybe they feel bad because they are leaving obligations, children, or financial problems behind and downloading some responsibility to their former spouse. Whatever the case, guilty spouses often make bad bargains. If you are dealing with feelings of guilt, make sure you get advice before you settle. Chances are that you may give up rights that you'll later feel regret over. If, after careful and objective consideration and third-party advice, you decide that the concessions are worthwhile and appropriate, then go ahead. But never make a deal because you feel bad for what's transpired. There's really no place for sentimentalism in settlement discussions.

There are, of course, many other reasons why parties sometimes make a quick and dirty settlement deal. The above examples are but a few obvious circumstances I see regularly. The point is that while this book is about non-litigious settlement solutions and finding happiness through the settlement process, you shouldn't rush into a bad deal for any reason.

6. Still Not Convinced to Seek Legal Counsel?

I know that lawyers, even divorce lawyers, do good work for people who are in trouble. In doing that job, some lawyers are wonderfully helpful, kind, caring, and considerate. Others, sadly, can be snotty, superior, annoying, and occasionally even dishonest.

The vast majority of lawyers, however, work long, hard hours and earn modest incomes. They face intellectual challenges on a daily basis which are, to many people, unimaginably complex and confusing. They are required to dispense legal advice which in turn requires a working knowledge of a variety of principles and disciplines, including accounting, psychology, and other fields. Lawyers work with challenging facts and difficult clients who are often not thinking straight, telling the truth, or even behaving well ... yet lawyers are expected to always achieve sensible, legal, and practical results. And it all must be done swiftly and with minimal expense. It's a really tough job.

This book isn't about lawyers, the hard job they do, or why they deserve to be liked. Rather, this book is about how to navigate your way through a separation or divorce, and how to use the legal system and the tools available within the justice system to survive that event financially, emotionally, and personally. To show the ways that this can be accomplished, it is necessary to understand something about the legal profession, and that's why I take extra time here to discuss the topic. It's not my job to restore faith in the work that lawyers do, but because I recommend that everyone see a lawyer at the outset of the separation and before signing any settlement, I want to establish some comfort level about the advice that's likely to be dispensed. Knowing that your family law lawyer is truly on your side and trying to help is critical.

The legal system is an easy target of criticism. Lawyers, like politicians, are the brunt of many nasty jokes. As professionals, lawyers have a colorful complexion and struggle for every earned ounce of community respect. The occasional bad lawyer has the instant fame necessary to contaminate an entire working population.

Yet despite it all, one of the proudest proclamations a parent can ever share is the announcement that their child was just admitted to law school! Similarly, even though everyone loves to hate the profession generally, when a friend or family member is in trouble, the most oft-heard advice is: "Better get yourself a good lawyer." This is almost always followed by, "Let me give you the name of my lawyer — he's the best — you better give him a call."

It's true. Everybody hates lawyers, yet everyone knows a great one. When there's trouble, everyone has a referral. Somehow, we all love to announce that we know the "best" lawyer for some particular assignment. It's almost like living next door to a celebrity!

What, you ask, does all this have to do with the theme of this book — and how does that tie in to the idea that there's a way to have a survivable separation? Well, let me explain.

Despite everything I have said about the law, its noble objectives, the fine people who work within the system, and the good, hard work that lawyers do, *divorce is a business*. The sooner we get that fact understood and out of the way, the better. If you don't truly understand what divorce really is, how it works, and what it costs, you cannot ever expect to control your own divorce competently.

If you really know what divorce is all about, you can navigate through the process with clarity and obtain a settlement that works for you and is financially intelligent.

Law is a business too, and in order for lawyers to support their families and continue to do good work, own homes, drive cars, and be productive, they need to be financially viable. A lawyer can't do any good for anyone if he or she is bankrupt — in fact, in many jurisdictions a lawyer who is bankrupt cannot practice law at all. So, as you approach the challenges in your separation, keep that in mind. Remember that the lawyer will do everything he or she can to help, but that it's going to cost something. It must cost money because no lawyer can work for free. Even though most good attorneys will offer a free initial consultation, it ends after the first visit and for good reason.

The legal process, and divorce laws in particular, can only function effectively if they are commercially sustainable. In countries without enough food, water, or good government, justice is illusory. Judges are not bribed in North America because we believe in the Rule of Law. We do not accept a system that does not have integrity and truth at the forefront.

Yet behind these noble objectives, we recognize that the system has to be practical, useful, and sustainable. People don't want to wait ten years for a marriage license or a divorce, and they demand rules and laws which make sense. They expect their judges to be bright, competent, impartial, and well trained. Obviously, there's a price for that.

Our law, when it functions well, makes economic sense. There is, as a result, a business aspect to the administration of justice.

Divorce law is business. The divorce business supports many characters and institutions, all vying for survival. From the law clerk to the court reporter; from the copy center worker to the mediator — all these people and institutions depend on the continued existence of a divorce system. Without litigation, many of these institutions would eventually cease to exist. Mediators might be able to earn their keep doing hospital litigation and car crash cases, but family law disputes are truly the bread and butter of a significant number of players in the justice business. It's an infrastructure that's easily miscalculated. Knowing how it works, and how interrelated it is, actually matters.

Contrary to what is commonly believed, lawyers, judges, mediators, and others do not need to create trouble to protect their jobs. A popular part of lawyer bashing is the allegation that lawyers fuel disputes in order to maintain pointless litigation — the theory being that if the lawyers can cause enough hard feelings, they'll make more money on fees. As I have stated earlier, this is nonsense. It's nonsense because almost every family law lawyer already has enough business to keep him or her busy for about 100 years. Lawyers don't need to incite trouble in failing marriages — there's already plenty of trouble out there. More importantly, however, family law lawyers don't get rich by litigating. In fact, they probably earn better money coming up with clever settlements that are satisfying and sensible. Causing trouble doesn't make family law lawyers rich, it makes the litigants poor. The divorce lawyer who litigates everything is likely working at a feverish pitch, accepting many risks, and making a reasonable income (but nothing more).

This truth can be used by separating spouses to their advantage. If you know that a separation settlement is an acceptable and remunerative way for lawyers to earn a legitimate living, you should ensure that your lawyer knows that settlement is what you want. It should be your key objective. Even though what's best for your lawyer isn't really supposed to figure in the process, the fact that you and your lawyer are on the same page can't hurt.

In the relationship with your lawyer, you are the client and the lawyer is the professional. He or she is expected and required to follow your instructions. Your instructions have to be lawful, of course, but a lawyer with a sensible client is a beautiful thing. A client who gives me reasonable instructions, asks me to settle for something fair, and cooperates in the process is a client who is easily pleased, and likely to save a lot of money. Of course, I charge for my service, but I charge less to a sensible client who is motivated to settle.

Clients who end up with a negotiated settlement are satisfied clients. A negotiated solution is not necessarily one that is delightfully pleasing to everyone — it's likely to be reached by concessions and compromises on both sides, and a little give and take. In order to increase the likelihood that your issues settle early and inexpensively, you should plan to approach the separation with settlement in mind. If you plan to meet with a lawyer, take some general advice, and then negotiate yourself, that's fine.

If you plan to negotiate with or through a lawyer, make sure that you provide instructions to your lawyer which are consistent with that. Tell your lawyer at the outset that you want to settle and that you are retaining him or her to negotiate a reasonable settlement. Do not allow your lawyer to think that litigation is your intention, or even that it's within the range of acceptable solutions. Make that clear from the outset.

Saying that you want to settle, hope to negotiate a compromise, and intend to be fair and flexible does not necessarily mean that you can settle. Obviously, if you're dealing with a hopelessly oppositional spouse, a party with outrageous demands, or needs that simply cannot be satisfied, you may end up in litigation despite everything. There is, however, no harm in sending the message that you want to settle. Remember that more than 90 percent of all cases do eventually settle for one reason or another.

7. When Don't You Need to Hire a Lawyer?

Just as there are many circumstances when you must get counsel, so are there circumstances and instances when you do not need a lawyer. Knowing exactly when you can manage without counsel and when you can avoid or limit your legal expense can be useful. The following sections discuss tasks in which you don't need to hire a lawyer to do the work for you.

7.1 When you tell your spouse you want to separate

Except in extremely rare circumstances, do not hire a lawyer to help you navigate through the twilight of your marriage or to announce your intention to end the relationship. Do that yourself. If this is not possible, get a counselor or psychologist to help, but don't use an attorney. Do it in person, during daylight, and absent any stimulants, contaminants, or intoxicants.

If you are uncomfortable about the prospect of making the announcement, or you are too emotional or otherwise not able to make the point for whatever reason, do it in writing. It may seem less humane, but perhaps that's unavoidable. A delivered letter is best, but email is fine too (although it may be hard to know if and when the message was received). Mark your communication "WITHOUT PREJUDICE" so that nothing in the communication can later be used against you.

If you are writing, also try to confine the announcement to that point alone — don't make offers or promises or describe your view of the law. That will come later. Now is not a good time to be discussing the future. You've just announced something that's probably quite disturbing. Keep the message short and simple. There's also nothing wrong with making the announcement on the phone, of course, but some consider it inappropriate.

In any event, do not hire a lawyer to send the message. That's unwise, uneconomical, and unlikely to encourage a sensitive reply. Of course, if you cannot make the announcement yourself because of a disability or fear of violence, it may be entirely appropriate to have counsel do the job for you.

7.2 When you are dealing with everyday minor family issues

Except in rare circumstances, do not ask your lawyer to write long-winded letters dealing with incidental matters. Lawyers are not usefully employed for the purpose of dividing the pots and pans, separating the garden furniture, or commenting on homework assignments for children. The details of everyday family governance cannot be handled by lawyers.

Although clients often ask me to deal with such matters, I almost always insist that the client communicate with his or her spouse in person (unless there's a personal restraining order or some other reason it's impractical). I tell my clients that lawyers are not needed for such issues, and that nobody can afford to have me do that.

In most parts of North America there are divorce coaches, parenting coordinators, and counselors to help parties resolve these disputes. Micromanagement by lawyers of the minutiae of household issues is a bad idea.

7.3 When you need financial advice

Do not use a lawyer to obtain financial advice. Although some lawyers may be willing to share their thoughts with you respecting the stock market, investment ideas, debt management and consolidation, and mortgage financing, that's really not their job. Nor are most lawyers competent or insured to give you that advice. Instead, talk to a financial planner, an accountant, a mortgage broker, or other impartial experts about your money woes.

Your lawyer should be paid to give legal advice and only legal advice. If you really need financial advice and don't know where to get it, your lawyer can probably give you a referral. Take the referral and get the advice from that source.

Having said all that, there may be some financial information that your lawyer will need and want to offer. For instance, let's say that my client owns a house with her estranged husband. She wants to keep the house. To do that, she will need to buy out her husband's interest in the family home. She needs to raise mortgage money to finance the deal, and doesn't know where to get started. I may be able to tell her what the lender will likely need, what it will cost to make the deal, and what documents she'll need to assemble. I can give her some general information about mortgage financing, prevailing rates, and the options available, but it would be wrong and inappropriate to do much more or give particular advice. Instead, I would and should refer the client to a bank, lender, or mortgage broker, so that the concept can be explored within a suitable professional environment. I might also refer my clients to other lawyers for tax problems, criminal law issues, or other matters, and I often send clients to accountants, actuaries, and even to doctors and counselors.

7.4 When you need psychological counseling

Don't mistake your lawyer for a counselor or an understanding friend. He or she is neither. Lawyers are not trained to give psychological advice, counseling tips, parenting guidance, or anything but legal advice. Make sure you keep in mind the role your lawyer is expected and required to assume.

8. Consider Other Dispute Resolution Options

If you and your spouse encounter conflict about incidental issues, consider dispute resolution options. Mediators can sometimes solve arguments over lesser issues with relative economy. Friends and family may also be useful.

That's particularly true when it comes to children's issues. Many separating spouses are easily able to find a consensus on finances, support topics, and other matters, but simply cannot agree on anything when it comes to the children. This is acutely so when it comes time to settle on the specifics of shared parenting.

When parents share the care and responsibility of children, co-operation is necessary to ensure a smooth transitioning between homes. This can become particularly tricky, sensitive, and confrontational when there are several children in several schools with a variety of extracurricular activities. Getting children to and from class, friend's homes, and sports and lessons can be a challenge in a nuclear family. In a divided home, the exercise can become the breaking point.

Fortunately, there are some excellent resources available to assist in most communities. Divorce coaches and parenting coordinators can help. Counselors may have useful tips and advice on the topic. For families with challenges of this type, it may be helpful to enlist the assistance of an arbitrator or other dispute-resolution person to help when there's conflict. There are many books written about the topic which may be helpful.

No matter your parenting challenges, you should try to remember that many fortunes have been lost fighting over parenting topics. That's because lawyers are not the best resource for solving custodial challenges. The legal expense incurred in a custody or shared-parenting battle can be greater than the cost of sending a young adult through college. Keep that in mind when estimating legal costs and the litigation system.

9. Circumstances in Which an Amicable Divorce May Not Be Possible

Regrettably, there are some limitations on the group of candidates who are eligible for an amicable divorce. Fortunately, the class of excluded candidates is small, but would certainly include spouses who are in a situation in which one spouse is a habitual liar, or is unstable physically or emotionally, or there is an issue of abuse.

There may be other circumstances in which the principle of a negotiated and simple divorce is unrealistic or impractical, but the following sections discuss the basics. Most people should be able to manage, so long as they're prepared, committed, and willing to give peace a chance.

9.1 The inveterate liar

If you have had the misfortune of marrying a person who is a lyin', cheatin' reprobate, this book probably won't solve your problems. In such circumstances, your interests would be better served by reference to a medley of country music hits and a quick trip to a litigation firm. While it's not necessarily the case that every spouse married to a liar will end up in court, it is almost universally true that where there's dishonesty about relevant matters, a lawsuit should be commenced.

It may be that, in time, after pleadings have been issued and your lawyer has prepared your case, the lying will stop, and you can negotiate from there. That is probably unlikely, but possible. What's beyond doubt is the prospect of an easy settlement in circumstances where there's no candor.

Having said that, not every kind of dishonesty will be fatal to the negotiation process. A spouse who has been untrue about matters of romance or fidelity may be entirely forthright about assets, liabilities, and children's issues. In such circumstances where the only lying is with respect to matters of the heart, it may not be necessary to hire a lawyer.

Let's say, for example, that your marriage has ended because your spouse has lost interest in you, and has developed a relationship with another person (e.g., a colleague at work). That news may initially be devastating, destructive, and hard to understand, but it does not necessarily mean that your spouse is incapable of the care of your child. It may mean that you are understandably cautious about issues of trust, and that you expect reassurances and need time to adapt. It may also mean that you will feel that the dishonest spouse can't be trusted to care for your newborn infant (particularly if your spouse is living with a new partner), but the fact of his or her infidelity does not mean that you cannot fairly negotiate a proper resolution of your family law issues, particularly if the children are older. In short, your spouse's infidelity to you is not necessarily a bar to talking your way to an amicable divorce.

However, where there is reason to believe that a spouse has been dishonest about topics that actually matter to the divorce itself, the fundamental underpinnings of negotiation may be absent. An example here is perhaps best.

Assume that your wife has told you she wants to end the relationship. You're anxious to resolve matters without fighting, and agree that the marriage is over. You meet to talk, and discover to your complete surprise that your wife has disposed of a significant portion of your family savings and raided the children's educational trust. You ask her about this, and she makes senseless excuses and won't come clean. Ultimately, you discover that she has developed a horrible gambling problem, and, coupled with a propensity for daytime drinking, has gone through about half the family portfolio.

In this circumstance, the trust is gone, but her breach pertains to a matter of some financial consequence. This isn't about her having a lover — it's about her honesty with respect to money management, the children, and family prosperity. If she refuses to fess up to her problem, won't come clean, and won't get help, it's going to be very difficult to negotiate a fair and balanced settlement. You may be able to achieve that objective in time, but until there's some sort of recognition, admission, and understanding of the problem, a smooth settlement is not likely.

If your spouse has been dishonest about accumulated income, expenses, or the use or disposition of savings, banking matters, or behavior respecting minor children, drug or alcohol issues, or any other issue of significance, consider contacting an expert lawyer soon.

However, if your spouse has been dishonest about your relationship, sex, romantic pursuits, personal satisfaction issues (i.e., residency, career aspirations, religious or cultural interests, or conflict with extended family), those issues probably will not interfere with frank and open discussion about separation. You may be able to find a solution despite those issues.

In essence, the principle here is that if there is an honesty issue in your relationship, you should ask, "Is this insincerity likely to contaminate our negotiations, or can I go forward with some certainty that my spouse will be honest in our discussions?"

9.2 The psychologically unstable spouse

If your spouse genuinely suffers from mental health issues, it's probably going to be difficult to sit down, have a nice chat, and negotiate your separation. That much, it would seem, is obvious.

Keep in mind that almost every separating spouse (at one time or another) will describe his or her other half as "deranged," "crazy," "whacko," or "unstable." It's human nature. One mechanism we use to protect ourselves from criticism is to tell our friends and family that our spouse is "cuckoo." It helps to make us feel safe and brings confidence. That does not necessarily mean that everyone accused of being crazy is, indeed, crazy. As we lawyers like to say, "There are always three sides to a story." Sometimes, good (balanced) people behave oddly when facing a divorce. Emotions run wild in the angst of separation, and some very stable people can sometimes act irrationally when it comes to love. Don't confuse that with mental illness.

However, if your spouse is genuinely suffering from some kind of mental illness (whether temporary, lasting, acute, chronic, or episodic), this book won't be of great assistance. An amicable divorce is predicated upon open and frank discussion of the issues that matter, with sound-minded and consenting adults. It presumes an equality of bargaining power, the absence of duress, and candor. If one of the parties is mentally ill, those basic ingredients are missing. In circumstances where you truly believe that there is a mental health issue at play, you will not benefit from any book. You probably need to see a physician or mental health counselor to address the problem, and you may need a lawyer.

9.3 The physically disabled or abused spouse

For similar reasons, if one or both spouses are disabled by reason of any physical difficulty, perhaps it's unlikely that you and your spouse can have a simple chat and make a deal. A disabled spouse, and indeed anyone who is unable to work or negotiate their issues freely by reason of limitation, presents special challenges. Because there is an inequality of bargaining power, great care must be taken to ensure that the disadvantaged spouse is properly represented and obtains full and frank disclosure. Even if everything looks fine and dandy on the surface, the disadvantaged party should have independent legal advice in the process. Only then can the bargain or contract have any realistic prospect of survival.

That doesn't mean, of course, that if your spouse is disabled you must stay married or start a lawsuit before separating. The law does not prohibit separation under any circumstances. Instead, the law entitles the disabled spouse to disclosure, representation, and consideration. Maybe the support scheme that's owed to a disabled spouse is payable at a higher amount or for a longer duration, but the law does not forbid separation.

10. An Important Note about Confidentiality and Privilege

When you meet with your lawyer, your discussions are private. They are governed by long-established and inviolate rules called "privilege" and "confidentiality." These rules and principles vary from place to place, but essentially remain constant in concept: The idea is that the discussions you have with a lawyer are private and cannot be shared with anyone unless special circumstances exist. The special circumstances generally permit or compel the lawyer to tell all whenever you consent to it, and (sometimes) whenever the disclosure relates to a matter of national security or a danger or crime that is about to be committed. Of course, any secret that is revealed in court proceedings is considered public, and so the tales you tell that are revealed in affidavits or testimony are also topics that are public.

Generally speaking, however, as a client, you can pour your heart out about your marriage or relationship and have a confident expectation of privacy. In most circumstances, you won't have to worry that the lawyer will share the details without your consent.

There's a great deal of law on this topic, and many important cases have focused on the concept and scope of privilege. Here, we cannot possibly get into the topic in any great detail, but it's important to understand the basic principle.

Even more important is an understanding of the limits of privilege. In this regard, the adage "What you don't know *can* hurt you" is applicable.

There is no privilege or confidentiality between you and your accountant. There may be a duty upon your doctor to preserve private communications, but similarly, there is no real protected or absolute privilege. The same goes for actuaries, business valuators, dentists, and other professionals.

If you have important aspects of your separation and divorce story which you want to keep absolutely private and confidential, discuss them with your lawyer but no one else. Do not discuss anything with your accountant, partner, dentist, or realtor unless and until you have discussed the matter with your lawyer. Your lawyer is your one true confidante in the world. It is important to be frank with your lawyer, and only your lawyer. Remember that your butcher, best friend, and even your accountant are compellable witnesses and can be forced to testify against you if need be, under fear of perjury.

11. Firing Your Lawyer

If you have retained a lawyer, and things aren't going as you hope, expect, or want, you need to do something about your situation. Cussing under your breath and complaining to friends is unlikely to increase satisfaction.

When you deal with a professional who has influence on your life, complacency is a bad idea. If things are not going your way, speak up.

Your lawyer is a professional. He or she expects criticism, and will likely be eager to hear from you if you are dissatisfied. If your lawyer does not want to hear your concerns, you definitely need new counsel.

In my practice, when someone is dissatisfied, uncertain about a situation, or just plain angry, I want the person to tell me. It's best if he or she can call or book an appointment. Sometimes, however, clients complain by email, and that too is a suitable method of expression. For some clients, it's simply too awkward to tell me to my face that I have said or done something that's dissatisfying, but they are comfortable expressing their worries in an email. That's okay.

I expect that most lawyers are like me on this point. They would far rather hear a complaint (whether it's fair or otherwise) than have a secretly unhappy client who festers and then fires. That's not good for anyone.

If you have a complaint to make about the speed of the process, the cost of the case, the staff, the result, the information, or any other aspect of the law, talk to your legal counsel. If you can't or won't call or write, find a way to make your worries known. If you can't do that, or if you have decided that it's time to move on, let the lawyer know immediately. The sooner that counsel puts his or her pen down, the better.

Again, it's best to do this in writing. Giving written notice of the termination of the relationship is good business practice. If it's necessary to later establish the date when you gave notice of termination, you'll have that in hand.

It's best not to be nasty, accusatorial, or abusive in the letter. This document may later become an exhibit if there's a challenge about the fees, and you don't want to regret your language on a subsequent occasion.

Be clear, be concise, and keep a copy of the letter. Tell the lawyer that you expect your file to be ready for pickup within one to five days, and explain that you will either pay the account balance due and owing or expect reimbursement for the remaining credit balance on the retainer. Either way, you need to square up with the lawyer and move on.

In most jurisdictions, if there's a dispute between the lawyer and the client over fees, there is a remedy available. In my area, an unpaid lawyer has a right to apply in the Supreme Court for relief. The lawyer can file an appointment to have a judicial officer hear evidence about the professional relationship and then render judgment on what amount, if any, is still owed. Similarly, a disgruntled client can make an application for an order in the same way. If the client believes that the bill is egregious, or that the amount claimed as owing is unfair, the client can ask the court to intervene and resolve the matter.

Many other jurisdictions have similar arrangements. Local bar associations and the law society can explain. If you have a dispute with a lawyer over fees, get that issue addressed, but do not tarry in the management of your case in the interim. Your dispute with former counsel should not stall the legal steps that need attention on your case. Also know that although the privilege (confidentiality) you enjoy with the lawyer during the relationship continues after you have parted ways, a lawsuit or other proceeding with respect to your accounts may constitute a waiver of privilege, and may open up some aspects of your case to others. Before challenging a lawyer's account in court, get advice from another lawyer. You don't want to have others looking through your litigation laundry just because you contested the former lawyer's bill.

5

Marriage and Separation Counseling

When you are facing a separation or divorce, you may, at some point, want or need counseling, or help from a psychologist.

You should know that there's no shame in reaching out for help. Many clever professionals seek counseling, and some psychiatrists, doctors, and philosophers themselves have the help of psychologists in their personal lives. You should be neither shy nor afraid to seek help.

Sometimes, the advice and information that's available from friends, the Internet, and the library simply is not adequate. In fact, I would say that the advice of friends and family members is usually dangerous, particularly on mental health issues.

Speaking with an impartial expert can provide comfort, relief, and insight. Often, all that's needed is a chance to vent or unburden yourself of the story, trauma, or upset that's bothering you. Other times, you may need help thinking slightly differently about matters. The counselor may have handouts, readings, or other resources that can help. The counselor may know what others like you have found helpful in the past.

Your relationship with a counselor is very different from the relationship you may have with a lawyer, but there is one striking similarity: Chances are that you will be divorced only once (or maybe twice) in your lifetime. Your lawyer will have handled hundreds or thousands of divorces. Most experienced counselors will have dealt with thousands of separating spouses. The sheer volume of experience that they bring to your family has undeniable value, and that's a resource from which you can benefit.

Counselors can be very helpful and, sometimes, their help can be instantaneous. Occasionally, all that's needed is an appointment or two. Sometimes the client only needs a little reassurance. Other times, there may be a need for ongoing therapy or treatment.

On a personal basis, I can tell you that I believe that any person facing a separation or divorce should see a counselor at least once. Truly, it's a nothing-to-lose and everything-to-gain proposition. Separation and divorce are extremely traumatic events for even the most stalwart and composed adult. Most counselors will tell you that a completely unmoved and unemotional divorcing parent is vulnerable to serious psychosocial trouble. Storing or bottling up emotions can be dangerous and harmful. Believe me, even if you can find a sympathetic, kind, and understanding lawyer who is willing and able to listen to your woes, lawyers are not trained to deal with such matters and are, in fact, professionally discouraged from hearing and entertaining stories about emotional issues. Get a counselor and go for a visit. If you don't benefit from it, don't return — but do make one appointment at least.

In my world, it's a bad sign if the separation is not emotionally challenging. If you don't worry, feel insecure, or demonstrate unusual apprehensions, you're probably hiding a more serious and possibly dangerous problem. If you are outwardly troubled, upset, nervous, and unsettled, you also should talk with someone. Either way, it's smart to see a counselor during separation.

Remember, too, that in the modern world, many employers offer extended health-care plans that provide coverage for such services. You should not feel embarrassed about asking your human resources department, manager, boss, or other workers about how to get coverage for a counselor. Nobody needs to know what it's all about. You may also find that your coworkers will respect you more and have greater understanding and compassion if they know you're getting expert help. At all times, it's up to you whether coworkers or your employers know anything.

Even if you have to pay for counseling yourself, you should get the help. Your mental health is not something you can afford to jeopardize. Don't take a chance with it — get some counseling whether you think you need it or not. If all is well, you can forget about the topic completely and carry on unscathed.

If you are having problems coping with the separation, a counselor or psychologist can be comforting and reassuring. A counselor who is skilled and experienced may also be able to give you other ideas and referrals to additional care providers, support groups, and private and community opportunities about which you may have no knowledge. Really, it's surprising how much your community may offer if you are willing to ask for help. Your counselor may even have collateral referral ideas about financial help resources and other groups and individuals who offer local assistance. Sometimes, counselors have better resources and referrals than your doctor, lawyer, or accountant.

Keep in mind that in every practice and profession, there are good and bad workers. Doubtless you have heard stories about doctors who are unkind, dentists who are rough, and accountants who lie about their golf score. No business, vocation, or profession is populated only by geniuses who are kind and courteous.

It's like that in the world of counseling too. So when you decide to see a counselor, know that the first person you contact may not be a perfect fit for you and your problems. Don't be discouraged by that. If you feel unable to establish a useful relationship with the counselor, try another. Finding the right expert can make all the difference in the world.

If you're going to see a counselor or a psychologist about your separation, you'll probably do most of the talking (initially). Eventually, you'll get some advice. Most counselors will tell you about therapies, techniques, and ways to think and act that may help you cope. Take that advice. Follow the instructions that are offered, and give the information an opportunity to be of benefit to you. Take the therapy or counseling for a reasonable period of time, and take the advice over weeks or months. No counselor or psychologist can wave a magic wand and effect improvement in a single visit. Give your caregiver a chance to help you. Even change that is initially of imperceptible value can be good later.

6
Getting Started

Once you have decided that your relationship has ended or must end, there are some important preparatory steps that must be taken. How, when, and where you begin these steps can make a huge difference in the range of possible outcomes you can expect. Here, in order, are some of the initial steps needing consideration:

1. Where, when, and how will you announce your intention to separate?

2. What are your objectives?

3. Who will be present during your discussions?

4. Have you prepared a statement of issues (or agenda)?

5. Have you prepared a statement of assets and liabilities?

6. What if your spouse refuses to accept the separation, or refuses to talk settlement?

The following sections will help you find answers to these questions.

1. Where, When, and How Will You Announce Your Intention to Separate?

Although this book isn't about how to leave your spouse, there is some common sense and practical advice on the topic. This I have gathered from listening to thousands of separating and separated couples over the years. I have learned what has worked for some people, and what definitely does not work.

When you plan to make you announcement, try to pick a sensible location. Offering your news in a crowded restaurant or at your parents' anniversary party is a bad idea. The best place to talk is at home when there's quiet and privacy. If there's going to be disappointment, surprise, or crying, it's only fair to deliver the news in familiar surroundings. Your home is a good location because there are opportunities for retreat.

I know that some separating spouses elect to make their announcement in front of a friend, family member, or a counselor. While that tactic may be reassuring for the person who is making the announcement, it's not often good for the recipient of the news. In some cases, it may seem like "ganging up" on the recipient — an emotional reaction that's unlikely to inspire calm discussion. Remember, separation, like love and sex, is an intensely private and personal matter. It should be announced in private.

If, however, you fear that the announcement itself may provoke an unpredictable, dangerous, or outrageous reaction, it may be wise to deal with the topic in the presence of others, or at least in a semipublic environment where risk can be minimized.

If you are dealing with a spouse who has either a history of violence or a propensity for dangerous behavior, you may want to reconsider whether to make any announcement at all. A better course may be to simply leave the home at some convenient opportunity and communicate your intentions later. You can do so by phone, by letter, through counsel, or in the presence of a friend or psychologist or counselor, but do not ever, under any circumstances, put yourself at risk. No relationship is worth a black eye, a broken nose, or worse. In fact, if you have reason to believe that your announcement could result in any misconduct at all, you may want to discuss your options with a lawyer *before* making plans of any kind. It may be that the concepts discussed in this book about separation techniques are inappropriate and inapplicable because of the risk element.

Make your announcement in the absence of the kids. They may figure importantly in negotiated terms later, but they do not need to be part of the adult discussion about the separation.

Once you have ascertained the best place to make your announcement, you need to consider timing. Generally speaking, and for obvious reasons, it's not wise to inform your spouse of your plans early in the morning or late at night. Do not raise the topic when alcohol has been or is about to be consumed. Try to find a sensible time (probably late afternoon or very early evening is best) in a quiet and private spot — such as your home — and you'll significantly increase the chances of receiving an appropriate response.

The question of "how" to announce your intention is quite a separate matter. In almost any relationship, the message is best delivered personally, in a calm, quiet, considerate, and respectful manner. Of course, reading about it in a book is one thing — delivering the message with sensible resolve may be quite a different matter.

It's not uncommon for the announcement to be an emotional event for both parties. Expect upset, crying, perhaps some anger, accusations, and expressions of disappointment. If you expect the worst, chances are you'll be pleasantly surprised when the deed is done. No matter what happens, you need to present the news in a measured way, with conviction and a firm but caring hand.

Don't be surprised if your announcement comes as no surprise at all. Sometimes, the decision can be a welcome relief. In many troubled relationships, the talk about separation can actually be quite welcomed.

Once, many years ago, I had a young lawyer in my employ. It wasn't going well. After about a year, it was obvious that the relationship just wasn't working, and it was going to be necessary to part ways. Amongst the partners, I drew the short straw when it came to making the announcement, and so I set a time to deliver the news. After several awkward rehearsals about what I would say, I called the young lawyer in and told him of the decision. I expected backlash, upset, anger, or complete horror, but instead, he let out a big sigh and said, "Oh, thank God." Secretly, he was finding the work torturous, but was afraid to give notice. Our decision to give him working notice was a welcome relief for both of us.

Sometimes, in a bad marriage, the decision by one party to call it quits can be a welcome change. While it's probably uncommon to have a friendly chat about the issue (at least initially), calm discussion about the how and why of separation can be unburdening and liberating.

There are many excellent books that describe the psychology of marriage and separation that you may want to read. Suffice it to say that it's my advice that taking a little care in making your announcement and being sensible about the "where, when, and how" can create a non-acrimonious environment that will continue as you go forward. Getting the separation process started on the right foot will serve you both well later.

Although it's not necessary to script your first discussion, it's generally wise to have some idea about the next step that's to be planned. Often, it is smart to make the announcement one day, and advise your spouse that you want to meet again two to ten days later, to discuss the issues.

Stick to your guns. Do not announce your intention and then back off while suggesting that you may be willing to discuss reconciliation. If you are truly willing to talk about fixing the relationship, don't talk about separation. You must make up your mind, and hold firm on your position.

Do not announce that you are leaving and immediately launch into an argument about support or asset division. Let the message sink in and give your spouse a chance to grapple with the topic generally before you move to specifics.

Don't say "it's over" and then walk out without communicating a plan. Leave your partner with some specific idea about what's going to happen next. Try to be nonconfrontational about it and do not threaten. Be clear and say something like the following, "I'd like to discuss our issues with you later, and I hope you'll agree that we can meet next Thursday to talk about what's going to happen." Having a next step clearly marked out will lessen the uncertainties and increase your partner's confidence in your plan. At least it will seem that you know where you're going.

2. What Are Your Objectives?

What are your objectives and what do you hope to achieve? Are there some issues which you can approach with flexibility, while others are inviolate and can only be resolved with one outcome?

Try to write down your objectives before your next meeting. Think about what you hope to obtain and achieve, and list them in priority. If your main objective is to get a fresh start, note that. If you want, above all, to emerge with certain assets and be free of certain debts, record those hopes. Even though it may be difficult or impossible to achieve all of your desires, you must know the objectives or there will be no real prospect of success.

In making your list, be fair to yourself, but don't be completely selfish. Try to realistically assess what your spouse might genuinely want and expect. Although you're probably parting ways because you can't get along, writing down a list of issues will help to focus your thoughts and organize your worries, even if you know that some topics will be confrontational.

If you know that your spouse will need and expect some money (at least for the interim) to support himself or herself, write that down. You can probably establish a sense of good faith by saying, "I know that you'll need some money, and I'm prepared to discuss that. It's probably a priority, so let's make that a focal point when we meet next."

You will need to prepare for your first meeting with your spouse. In doing that, you should consider in advance which topics you may be willing to "give" on — that is, those issues in which you can offer concessions or compromises. If you can identify the matters capable of compromise from those about which you want to take a steadfast or stalwart position, you'll be off to a good start.

On the one hand, it may make perfect sense to set out your nonnegotiable issues at the very outset. For instance, if you're willing to be flexible on money matters, but consider anything less than shared parenting a nonstarter, it may make sense to say so early in the discussion. Maybe your spouse will be more likely to settle into a calm discussion if he or she understands what really matters to you, and appreciates that you may be willing to show latitude on some topics but not on others. On the other hand, it may be that you want to hold back some cards until after the process is well under way. If you reveal all your compromises at the first discussion, you won't have anything to offer up later if the bargaining becomes heated. Some lawyers use this technique to significant advantage. In a more friendly and casual discussion, such tactics may have no place. You'll have to judge for yourself, based on the atmosphere that exists at the time of the discussion.

3. Who Will Be Present During Your Discussions?

When you begin your planning, you will also want to consider whether the discussions will be held in private or whether it may be wise to meet in the presence of a friend, family, religious leader, neighbor, or some other mutually respected individual. Again, there are no rules about who can and should be present for the discussions, but common sense should prevail.

Make sure that you do not align yourself with persons who will only be supportive of your position. Don't bring along a "helpful" pal who has no respect for your spouse and won't be sympathetic. Usually, it's best to come alone, but if you must bring someone, choose a sensible, calm, and compassionate friend or relative.

4. Have You Prepared a Statement of Issues (or Agenda)?

If you come to the first meeting armed with some sort of formal presentation or documentation, you'll probably be perceived as unfeeling or weird. Having said that, it's good to know what topics need to be addressed and what issues should be priority topics. Organizing these in your own mind before your meeting is a wise practice. For your second meeting you should have a plan.

Write down the concerns you have. Write all of the issues down. Wait 24 hours, and then review them again. This time, add priority number assignments to each issue. Leave the list for another 24 hours, and then take a final look. As you think about it, and repeatedly visualize the list, several things will happen. First, you may find that some of the topics which at first seemed very important probably don't matter as much. Second, you will probably discover that you don't need the list anymore. Once you have written down your worries, you will be able to clearly remember what needs to be addressed even without the list.

If that doesn't happen, or if you are just one of those people who works better with notes, prepare a short list of topics or an agenda for your discussion. Keep in mind that if you write this material down and refer to it (or are discovered looking at it), your spouse will probably want to have a look. As a result, the list should be clinical and free of any comments or notations that are likely to cause trouble. Sample 1 shows what an agenda may look like.

Obviously, this is a preliminary draft that's an offer for guidance only. Your actual agenda may be very different. Keep in mind,

SAMPLE 1
Separation Agenda

(Dave and Sally, June 5, 2011)

1. Dave moves out of the home (when, where to, etc.).

2. Finances afterward (bank arrangements, support, mortgage, and car payment).

3. The next step — a meeting with a mediator? Should we exchange written offers? Understanding what matters to Sally.

4. If we are able to agree: Who will prepare the separation agreement?

5. Other issues: Our wills, the dog, and savings.

however, that for the first meeting (or two) you should not be overly ambitious. There may be hard feelings, tears, and upset. Don't show up with an agenda at the initial announcement, but do have a plan for the subsequent meetings. Don't load up your agenda with 100 contentious topics. For instance, don't start with a real tear-jerker topic, such as, "How do we explain to Grandma that we don't love each other?" However, don't skirt the issues. If one of you is moving out, put that on the agenda and deal with it. There's no point pretending everything's okay.

Plan to have more than one meeting, and stage the issues. Don't raise custody in the first meeting if you know it's going to be contentious. However, since interim support (the immediate money issues) needs redress at the outset, put that on the first agenda. Get it out of the way, establish some good faith, and then move forward. Make sure you honor the commitments and promises you make.

5. Have You Prepared a Statement of Assets and Liabilities?

A statement of assets and liabilities is another key part of your early preparation. This document is a list of what you own and what you owe. For most families, it's one page.

Start with the assets. Be as specific as you can, but use common sense. If you are like most families, the balance in your checking account changes day to day, so don't worry about pinpointing that. Instead, focus on real and fair market values of all the big ticket items. Do include vehicles, but don't include pots and pans. Sample 2 shows you what a statement of assets and liabilities may look like.

SAMPLE 2
Statement of Assets and Liabilities

ASSETS		
Description	**Detail**	**Value**
House: 123 Main Street	Jointly owned	$350,000
Dave's car	2005 Nissan	$10,000
Sally's car	2006 Ford	$11,000
Dave's savings	Insta-rich fund	$22,000
Sally's savings	Various stocks	$9,000
Household furnishings	Miscellaneous	$10,000
19-foot ski boat	Jointly owned	$6,000
LIABILITIES		
Description	**Detail**	**Amount**
Mortgage on home	Joint debt	$220,000
Dave's car loan	Bank	$3,000
Sally's credit card	Visa	$2,500

The purpose of this list is to ensure that the parties know and appreciate their situation. Although it would be unusual for one spouse to be unaware of the basic information, it's not uncommon for separating spouses to be surprised by some of this information. I sometimes encounter spouses who have no idea what's owed on their mortgage (and some spouses who don't even know that they have a mortgage). Setting out the basic information in writing early in the discussions is a good idea. It costs nothing to be clear, and eventually this information may form the basis of an agreement and amicable separation. At some point, you are going to be required to warrant that you have accurately disclosed all, so you might as well get it out and on the table at the outset.

6. What If Your Spouse Refuses to Accept the Separation, or Refuses to Talk Settlement?

You may find at your first meeting that your spouse refuses to accept your announcement, and won't talk about or cannot cope with the prospect of settlement. What then?

First and foremost, recognize that the news you are delivering may be predicted, expected, and welcome relief, or it may be a shocking and devastating revelation. Either way, the reaction you get initially may not necessarily mean very much about what's going to happen in the coming weeks. People react and respond to sudden news in different ways. If your spouse shows initial disbelief and horror, don't panic. The news and reality of what's happening may simply need a few days to sink in. Also note that an apparent initial calm by your spouse does not necessarily mean that there won't be a firestorm of trouble next month.

All you can do is present the information that you have, as plainly and kindly as possible. Tell your spouse that you are committed to resolving the outstanding issues simply and with compromise, and that you hope that it will be possible to do that without litigation. However, do not be surprised if your best laid plans do not, at first, attract that same cooperative attitude. You should expect resistance and upset, and be pleased with anything better.

Be patient, but not too patient. You should set a time line for resolution of the issues. Be considerate and thoughtful, and recognize that different people move at different speeds through life. Give your spouse time to ponder, but don't wait forever. It should take a few weeks to a few months to resolve matters (with or without lawyers). Don't make the separation your life's work.

There may be circumstances, however, where it's just not possible to move swiftly. That may occur not because of any delay on your part or because of your spouse, but simply because other parties and information are not immediately available. For instance, if you need to have your home appraised, your business valued, or if other income or asset details are missing, you may face a time lag while other persons perform various functions. That delay may be unavoidable.

Similarly, if you engage a lawyer for advice and there are tricky legal issues relating to tax, asset valuation, or other sensitive topics, the lawyer may need a little time to gather information, research a point of law, or confer with other experts.

Either way, these steps take weeks, or perhaps a month or two, but not 6 or 12 months. So if you have been waiting for a lawyer or an accountant for more than a couple of weeks, call. Ask what's going on, what is causing the delay, and ask if there's anything you can do to move things forward. Finally, ask for a date when you can expect the answer or conclusion you're waiting for, and then write it down on a calendar or enter it into a day planner. Try not to annoy or hassle your lawyer or accountant, but do be responsible and punctual. Hold your helpers to the time estimates they provide.

7. Record Your Progress — The Separation Agreement

Keep in mind that the object behind your discussions — the purpose you are communicating — is resolution of the outstanding issues. What you want, more than anything, is an agreement. When you reach an agreement, you can record it in writing and call it a separation agreement. That is a document (or contract) that will govern your parting of ways.

There are numerous rules and principles about separation agreements — about what should be included, how the terms should be described, and whether the document should be filed. Many of these rules vary slightly from one jurisdiction to another. The rules which apply to separation agreements made in Alaska may not be the same as those in Quebec. For that reason, it will be important for separating spouses to speak with a local lawyer before signing the separation agreement. You won't be doing that to see if the lawyer can rewrite your contract, but you will be looking for reassurances that the contract is jurisdictionally valid and will be upheld.

In most of Canada, the rules are fairly consistent. For that reason, my other book (simply entitled *Separation Agreement*, which is available from Self-Counsel Press) offers general advice and a sample agreement. The information contained in that book probably won't apply in most areas of the United States, but the general concepts have some relevance, so I will repeat them here:

- A separation agreement should be in writing.

- It must be signed (executed) to be enforceable.

- It must be executed by consenting adults who are competent and sober and not oppressed or coerced into settlement, and the execution should be witnessed by two independent persons.

- The facts and principles on which the agreement is based must be true (if one spouse has lied about assets, for instance, the agreement may be void).

- The agreement should be complete. It should deal with all relevant issues, including children's residency, visitation (access) and guardianship, support for children and spouse (if applicable), and the division of property.

- The agreement should be fair. A hopelessly one-sided agreement, or one which is otherwise incomplete, incomprehensible, or improper, is likely to be set aside.

- Both parties should keep an original signed copy of the agreement.

These are the very basic rules about separation agreements. I think that these basic rules are probably universally true. Specific detailed rules and principles, as stated, may vary from one place to the next.

Americans have the luxury of Internet access to many do-it-yourself separation resources. Most of these (at least most of the ones that I have seen) are good resources, which contain helpful information and useful tips. In Canada, there are fewer resources, although a good sample agreement is contained in the Self-Counsel Press publication *Separation Agreement*. I think it's good partly because it's my book, but also because my staff and I take care to update it regularly and ensure that the latest version is useful and appropriate.

Whether you live in the US or Canada, make sure to use the available materials as a precedent or sample only. No do-it-yourself kit is completely adequate for every circumstance and every family. Generally speaking, the kits are good for simple separations in which the parties have few assets, a few liabilities, and are in general agreement. If that's not the case, the general utility of these publications is less certain.

For less than $35, you can purchase a precedent agreement that is probably substantially accurate for use in your state or province. At the very least, the kit will show you what an agreement should look like and will demonstrate the way in which you need to deal with the topics at hand. Either way, you must see a local lawyer before you sign anything, so the suitability of your precedent can be checked.

As I have stressed repeatedly throughout this book, you don't need to have a lawsuit to settle your separation issues. However, of paramount significance is the need to have counsel at several stages in the process and in certain circumstances. I won't repeat all that here except to say this: You must see a lawyer before you sign any legally binding agreement. You must take the initiative to sit down with counsel, either for a free interview or for a paid hour of advice, and ask for help *before* you sign your agreement. If you do not do that, you may be in for a world of trouble and upset later.

I have also mentioned that the agreement must be complete. I say that because many separating spouses think that they have handled everything appropriately, only to find out later that the house transfer was not concluded, or that the children's passports were overlooked. If the separated spouse is still cooperative, that kind of oversight may be no big deal. However, if there's trouble, or if the separated spouse is overseas, or dead, it may be a big problem. For that reason, I encourage parties to ensure that their contract — their separation agreement — is complete and deals with all issues. That is not to say, however, that issues cannot be addressed during the process on a piecemeal basis.

Sometimes, spouses find that they can resolve one, two, or ten issues, but they can't solve everything. In some cases, that's because the remaining issues are too contentious, tricky, or upsetting. I see this often with parents who are able to divide their assets and settle support, but cannot agree on where young Johnny should live. In other cases, I find that parties are able to resolve everything respecting the kids, but they are unable to settle the issues regarding the division of contents in the home or the support. People become stalemated for different reasons.

There are times parties cannot resolve one or two remaining issues simply because of some independent fact or unknown that is delaying the resolution. For instance, perhaps the spouses can agree generally that the proceeds of a car crash settlement should be divided, but they do not know how much is likely to be received or when. They may be able to resolve the issue when the settlement occurs, but without knowing how much is at stake, they cannot agree. Still another example would arise where the parents of a college-bound teenager do not know what costs will be upcoming for young Johnny's first year. If he's accepted to the London School of Economics, the costs may be stratospheric, but perhaps he'll only gain admission to a local junior college. If money is an issue, and the parents cannot agree on how to share the expense (no matter what it is), they may find themselves at a standoff over this issue alone.

In such circumstances, it may not make sense to wait. The agreement on the topics which are agreeable can be prepared, reviewed with counsel, and if appropriate, that document can be signed. Somewhere in the contract, the parties should describe the issues which they cannot resolve, and then they can explain how they have, nonetheless, agreed to address the issues when further facts are known or at some future date. As long as the language of the paragraph is clear, that should suffice.

The point here is that recording progress on settled issues is proper, even if you can't solve everything. Do your best to settle every topic, but if that's just not possible, record your agreeable terms as best you can and then move on. In the end, you will need a comprehensive resolution, but recording successes along the way is fine.

7

Disclosure

Disclosure is critical. In one recent Supreme Court case in my jurisdiction, a judge commented that "nondisclosure is the cancer of matrimonial litigation."

There can be no fairness, no justice, and no finality in any separation agreement that is negotiated in the absence of full, complete, and accurate disclosure. It simply cannot happen.

Almost every week, I encounter a client who seems to be breaching this rule. Despite my oral and written demands for candor in the disclosure process, I regularly encounter clients who think that, for whatever reason, they are exempt from disclosure rules. Typically, I tell these clients about the rules one more time, point out the risks of their behavior, and sometimes I simply terminate the retainer and fire the client. I do that because I really don't have time for a client who doesn't respect the basic rules of the process.

1. Nondisclosure Is a Crime

Sometimes I encounter a client who thinks that if he or she does not tell all, there can be big savings. This client, typically not a fraudster or outright liar, will convince himself or herself that if the little bank account in Washington is "forgotten," there can't be any harm done. If, somehow, it's discovered later, the remorseful apology will include comments like "oops," or "sorry, I forgot about that."

I suspect that during my career, I have actually acted for several hundred of these "concealing" clients, and I'll probably never know who they are. Some of them have likely saved considerable sums of money and protected untold assets that may have considerable financial worth.

The concealing clients have, however, left something behind with me when they left my office. Every one of them has left a paper trail contained in a file in my firm, awaiting revelation, review, and reconsideration. That's because in every American and Canadian jurisdiction I know of, nondisclosure of any material asset or liability will permit, and indeed invite a subsequent court to review the settlement and vary it, sometimes retroactively. Usually, there are significant penalties for nondisclosure.

When I am discussing this situation with clients who may be wavering about compliance with the disclosure rules, I tell them about this. I explain that if they have overlooked and not disclosed assets (even "little" stuff), they are inviting a subsequent court to reconsider the settlement. These hidden assets, if they are worth anything, almost always turn up somewhere, somehow. After all, an asset is worth nothing unless it's used.

Sometimes the asset is later revealed in a sloppy conversation made years after the settlement in the comfortable afterglow of resolution. The information gets back to the sore and cheated spouse, and before you know it, there's a new Supreme Court action.

Still other times, the information about the asset comes back via a child, common friend, business associate, realtor, banker, doctor, or neighbor. On occasion, it's the use of the asset that results in the revelation. I once acted for a wife who "gave up" her case because her spouse was quite clearly penniless, until about two months later, she saw him by happenstance, driving a new Jeep. A review of the license plate revealed ownership (acquired at a time prior to settlement), and before you knew it, my bailiff had seized the Jeep for sale.

The rule here is that if you have "forgotten" a small account in Washington, a little investment overseas, a boat that's shared with a friend, or an undistributed inheritance in France, you are very likely to be found out in due course. Someday, some way, your cheat will be known, and you will have to pay. Even if nobody during your living years finds out, an asset of any significant worth which falls into your estate is likely to be revealed to your heirs (and the court), and so eventually, all will be known.

Nondisclosure is a crime. The crime of nondisclosure in matrimonial matters is rarely punishable under criminal law, but it is often punished as contempt of the court. This can result in incarceration (jail). I know that because I have seen it happen.

2. Undervaluing Assets

Another type of breaching client is the party who thinks it would be clever, ingenious, unimportant, or otherwise somehow acceptable to disclose all the assets, but "fudge" on valuation. This rarely happens where counsel are engaged or if the asset is of substantial value, but it does happen, and with some frequency.

If lawyers are involved in the division of assets having significant worth, and the value is not easily ascertained, it's common to seek an appraisal by an expert. In that case, even though the expert's valuation is only an educated guess, there is *some* evidence of value. If one party is unhappy with the opinion, he or she can hire her own expert and get another valuation. Eventually, the worth of the asset will be known with some degree of certainty.

In many cases, however, lawyers are not involved and parties try to settle everything without counsel or accountants in an attempt to avoid unnecessary expense. Saving a few hundred dollars on legal advice in such circumstances is like asking your hairdresser to check your parachute!

If counsel is not engaged, and accountants play no role, parties will themselves make representations about value, relying on the honesty and integrity of the other party and their own sense of things. This can be a risky approach.

In some cases, a spouse who is undervaluing an asset will do so deliberately, in an attempt to fool the unsuspecting spouse into accepting an artificially low estimate of value for an asset that can later be retained by the undervaluing party, or sold subsequently for gain.

Many times in my career I have seen this tactic backfire completely. Take, for instance, the example of the husband who undervalues the RV. In this hypothetical situation, the husband hopes to keep the motorhome because he loves it and he knows that his wife won't drive it. He tells her it will be hard to sell. He says it needs some work, and must be insured. It probably has value in the $60,000 range, but to his separated wife, he deliberately represents that it's worth $30,000. He offers to pay her $15,000, and says he'll "take it away without delay." She doesn't want a fight, doesn't know what RVs are worth, and so she thinks about agreeing to that. She thinks his valuation is low, but she just wants the case to end. The husband puts the proposition into a written separation agreement, and she goes to the local lawyer for advice.

In this scenario, the lawyer is no RV broker, but he knows a few things. He asks the wife for details about the RV (model, year, size, mileage) and then makes a couple of calls. Or maybe he spends five minutes on the Internet. Either way, within five minutes he's ascertained that the value of the RV is significantly more than $30,000. He sees that the husband has made that representation in writing, and so he knows that if he goes to court, he can use this to his advantage. He can show the judge that the husband has made material misrepresentations to the wife as an inducement to settle. Now the lawyer can ask the judge for an order that his client (the wife) be at liberty to take ownership and possession of the RV for the price the husband offered to pay her ($15,000). She obtains that order, calls the RV consignor, and sells the motorhome, making herself a tidy little profit.

In this case, if the husband had been forthcoming about value, he wouldn't have had this problem. He might have, as an alternative to misleading his wife, said this:

"You and I both know that the motorhome is worth more to me than to you. I can drive it, and I like it. I want it. I'm prepared to take it at slightly more than fair market value. You don't really want it, and aren't interested in driving it. It only makes sense for me to buy your interest in the motorhome.

"If we sell it ourselves, we will have to insure it, market it, and show it. Somebody has to spend time cleaning it up, supervising every inquiry, and haggling with a buyer.

"If you call a few dealers, and spend some time on the Internet, I think you'll find that market value for that RV is probably about

$60,000 in a perfect world. That means that in the perfect world, your best case scenario sees you recovering a maximum of $30,000 for your half interest. I'm prepared to pay you $20,000 right now, and take it away. What do you say?"

That's a better approach. The husband gets a deal, and the wife gets instant cash. More importantly, neither of them is in breach of the law, and there's no disclosure problem.

Sometimes, however, the undervaluation issue is less obvious and perhaps unintentional. A good example is with respect to employer-sponsored pensions.

Most governments, corporations, and institutional employers offer long-term employees pension plans that pay benefits upon death or retirement. Although there are many different types and kinds of pension funds, they all (usually) share some of the same features:

- they are contributed to by the employee (biweekly, monthly, or annually);

- the employer also makes some sort of contribution (often a percentage of pay);

- they are usually protected from tax while being saved, and taxable in the hands of the recipient if and when received; and

- they are, in most jurisdictions, divisible family assets that should be shared upon separation.

A pension of this type is a couple of things. At any moment in time, it consists of a known and identifiable savings fund with a specific arithmetic value. In addition, the pension is also an entitlement to a future stream of income. The stream of income is of significant value, but that value or worth is not always immediately ascertainable.

For almost all separating spouses, the worth of the entitlement to a future stream of income is something that only a professional, trained economist (called an "actuary") can explain. Actuaries are able to give opinions about the present value of a pension by reference to the saved portion of the fund and the terms and conditions of the plan, but only if they are given the opportunity to review the particulars. They will then use a variety of facts and tools (including life expectancy tables) to estimate the present value of the fund. The cost of an actuarial valuation of a pension is usually between $500 and $1,500. Given that many long-term workers have more stored equity in their pension than in their home, it's critical to proceed with extreme care when dividing a pension. It's often necessary to engage an actuary, and it is almost always necessary if one party is going to buy out the interest of the other.

In any event, the circumstance of nondisclosure that arises from undervaluing which I am describing here happens in respect to pensions because the parties may not know or appreciate the value of the fund. That's because many spouses do not understand their pension fund. When they look at the value of the fund, they look to the most recent contributor statement. Somewhere on that document is a place where the employee's contributions are probably described. The uninformed employee will take the value based on the accumulated contributions of the pensioned spouse only, without considering the employer's contributions or the contractual obligations of the employer to pay the pension benefits over time.

For example, if I have worked for ABC Ltd. for 20 years and contributed $500 per month to my pension (from my income of $7,000 per month), I will have put away $6,000 each year. Over 20 years, with interest on the saved portion, my contributions on my contributor statement may be $180,000. If I then separate from my wife, and represent that her half-value interest in my pension is $90,000, I may be grossly understating the value of my entitlement (depending on the pension itself, my age, and other factors). If I do that inadvertently or because we are both ignorant as to the true value, the "undervaluation" may not be particularly nefarious or contemptible, but the result is the same. The deal made on the basis of faulty information is always a bad deal, and is very likely reviewable. (For more information about pensions, see Chapter 8.)

Those are but two examples of undervaluation which commonly arise in matrimonial cases. There are, of course, variations on these themes, and lesser and greater examples of offenses. I have seen cases, for instance, where a party has simply left out a valuable piece of property, thinking or hoping that the omission will be overlooked or the asset forgotten. Sometimes there's success in that, I suppose, but it's never proper to do that, and it's never fair. If you want to lie and cheat your way to an advantageous settlement, you probably don't need to read any more of this book. Instead, you should probably get yourself a criminal law lawyer on retainer and go to confession. Nothing I can tell you in this book is going to correct that attitude.

Disclosure problems are occasionally insignificant and sometimes inadvertent. This does not mean that parties should not make their best efforts to get it right.

3. Disclosure: Common Sense Principles

The duty of disclosure does not mean that it's critical in every case to list every pot and pan, all the bedding, and the garden tools. Rarely will a complete review of incidental household chattels be necessary. Let common sense be your guide.

Listed below are some common sense principles that may be of assistance:

- The parties should make a good and honest effort to get all the assets and all the liabilities listed with complete candor at the outset.

- The parties should then review the list prepared by the other party and make any necessary or proper adjustments.

- If a dispute exists about whether an asset or liability is or is not properly included, that dispute should be resolved one way or the other before the settlement negotiations continue. If you cannot agree on what you and your spouse owe and own, you are likely not ready to settle the big topics.

- If there is a dispute about the value of any asset, gather proof. Do not simply accept the representation of your spouse. That does not mean that you must distrust your spouse, but be smart. With the Internet resources that currently exist, there's simply no reason for settling without some independent evidence about value.

If your discussions occur early on after a recent separation, you will likely have a good idea of what the assets and debts are. It's easy to know, because the relationship recently ended. If you don't discuss these issues for months or years, it may be more difficult to figure out what values existed at the time of separation, and a fair division may lead to more complex inquiries.

4. Situations in Which Disclosure Is Not Simple

There may be cases in which disclosure is not simple. In some relationships, one party takes care of the family business, the banking, and the finances, and the other spouse is largely in the dark. In many families, there is a division of the familial responsibilities, for better or worse. It's not only in traditional/conventional families that one spouse looks after all the finances while the other spouse cares for the kids and home. There's much more to it in the modern world.

I once acted for an intelligent man who worked for wages in an industrial company owned by his parents. In his free time, he practiced his musical talents and busied himself with other activities. His wife was a banker and an astute businessperson. She looked after all the family finances because she was good at it, enjoyed it, and by default. He certainly could have taken an interest and played a role, but it was not his "thing" and he chose to learn nothing about it.

When they separated, it took some time to get him up to speed. As a parent who had never taken any real interest in understanding the family financial picture, he was completely unable to explain the family asset situation, their pension issues, or the state of affairs regarding debts, credit cards, and the like. In time, all was revealed, and the matter was ultimately settled on fair terms, but the disclosure issue was very worrisome at the outset.

Separating spouses need to know their family business. An uninformed spouse is more likely to be victimized by an improvident settlement.

If the separation discussion happens months or years after the end of the relationship, there may be some explaining to do. For instance, in the aftermath of a marital split, spouses will sometimes take on new financial obligations in an attempt to set up a new home, and build a new life as a single person or single parent. It costs money to separate, and so new loans, credit card debt, or family obligations may have arisen in the aftermath. These must be disclosed, even if the debtor has no intention of asking the former spouse for contribution or indemnity with respect to the debt. It is important to list these debts so that they are known and identified, and then they can be dealt with. If one spouse has taken on new debt for new furniture and accepts that financial responsibility, that's fine.

In the disclosure description, use plain language to explain these things; for example, "Wife's new furniture, purchased at Smith's Gallery, post separation." Next, list the debt that goes along with it: "Wife's MasterCard debt for $3,200, respecting purchase of furnishings at Smith's Gallery." Once that's disclosed, it can be agreed that "The wife's furnishings, purchased at Smith's Gallery post separation, and the wife's MasterCard debt incurred for that purpose, shall be and will hereafter remain exclusively her asset and liability. The wife agrees to seek no compensation or contribution from the husband in respect to that debt, and the husband agrees to make no claim to ownership or possession in respect to the furnishings."

The essence of the rule here is that every asset of any significant value and any debt of significant consequence should be disclosed. Then, when the agreement describes how the assets and liabilities are to be shared, care can be taken to ensure that *all* the assets and liabilities are divided and dealt with in the agreement and that no loose ends remain.

One way to cross-check for completeness is to carefully examine the list of assets and liabilities that you have prepared (see Chapter 6) and ask yourself if each and every one of the items on that list has been dealt with in the agreement. If not, why not? In general, any and every asset and liability should be disposed of in your agreement, one way or the other.

8

Assets

This chapter discusses issues surrounding assets such as the family home, pensions, property transfers, and family businesses. It also includes information on how to resolve liability issues in regards to transferring assets.

1. The Family Home

In many family law cases, the issues surrounding the family home are particularly contentious. That, I suppose, is to be expected. Over time, people (particularly people with children) tend to become attached to their homes. They think of them as their safe place or sanctuary, and have recorded fond memories and other symbolic connections with the place they live. Over time, as children grow and familiar surroundings, neighbors, and other comforts develop and offer reassurance, the resistance to change becomes even more pronounced. When a separation occurs, it's often the case that the biggest battle is over "who gets the house."

Bumper sticker logic seems to creep into the analysis, and tearful spouses will tell me that they don't want to leave their home, citing, instead, propositions such as:

- "It's not our house, it's our home."

- "It's the only home the kids have ever known."

- "If I lose that house, I lose everything."

As sentimentally sound as these utterances may be, they are absolute bunk when it comes to family law.

There may be many good reasons for staying in a house. Proximity to schools, friends and support networks in the area, market uncertainty, and other reasons come to mind. Having said that, when you separate, there are many reasons the logic of owning a particular home may not figure in the new equation.

When you separate, you are *each* entitled to some of the equity in the home, unless there are very good reasons why that's not so or some weird fact or circumstance exists which alters the general rule. As a result, it is usually unfair for one party to hold the other hostage — both parties have a reasonable expectation that they should have access to a share of the equity in the home. If you want the home and your spouse wants some equity, you will have to buy out his or her share. It's usually just that simple.

Sometimes, that's not possible. Because of strained financial circumstances, the spouse who wishes to remain in the home may find it difficult to raise the necessary financing. Occasionally, that can be addressed through support issues. Will alimony pay the monthly installment? Can a friend or family member help? Can the staying spouse refinance with a wealthy guarantor? Is there a sister or brother who would be willing to become a partner in the house, "taking out" the interest of the departing spouse by payment and replacing the spouse on title? Could the spouse sell the home to a friend and stay on as a tenant (perhaps with a right to repurchase at a later date)? These and other options can and should be explored.

Sometimes, however, the fight over possession of a home is acute even when the parties are tenants, or living in leased premises. Arguments over mere possession of temporary accommodations can be profoundly hard fought.

When lawyers dispense advice about this topic, it's often the same. The common principle is: If the parties cannot agree on what to do, sell it and split the proceeds. If the property is rented, both parties may need to move.

It's easy for lawyers to sit back in their offices and dispense advice about the disposition of the home. We are asked, in our roles as independent counsel to be impartial, objective, and to impart only practical and sensible advice that is based on law and logic. In such circumstances, it is easy to offer simple advice. In many families, that advice has practical worth. A quick sale (even at a fire sale price) can sometimes save the parties thousands in legal expense and untold suffering and argument.

However, sometimes it's not that simple. In many families, arguments arise because the parties have not carefully considered the multiple advantages relating to occupation and possession of the family home. Sometimes, these go well beyond simple economic considerations. A list of some of the factors might include the following:

- How long have the parties lived in the area?

- Is the home close to work, extended family, or amenities?

- Can the kids walk home from school, or to the caregiver's place?

- Is the area safe?

- What's the cost of alternate accommodation (i.e., if this house is sold, will the family be forced out of the area)?

- What's special about the house? Is the yard huge? Is there a special needs child who's adverse to change? Are the neighbors supportive?

- What's the equity situation? If the house is sold, will the parties both be effectively shut out of the market and forced into tenancies?

- Does one party have an overwhelming claim to possession based on child-care circumstances, special needs, or other factors?

- If there's a sale, what (in practical terms) will happen to the proceeds? Can the parties agree on a division and move on, or is the money likely to fuel more fighting and legal expense?

- Does either party have a legal or other claim to more than half the proceeds?

- How is the local realty market? If the market is slow, are the parties going to suffer?

- What is the condition of the home? Are significant repair bills likely to arise in the near future?

- Can one party afford the financing necessary to buy out the other party?

- Is a delayed or deferred sale likely? Are the kids very nearly grown or graduated?

- Will the court direct a sale if the parties do not agree?

These and several other questions can and should be asked in any situation where the parties are unable to agree on the point.

Keep in mind that it's very easy for a judge to order a sale. Creative financing options and plans that involve action "outside the box" are unlikely to be entertained by a court. In short, more options and alternatives exist for spouses who are cooperative.

One option that's often overlooked is a delayed payout. Under this kind of scheme, the departing spouse does one of two things:

1. He or she transfers title to the remaining spouse, but then takes a mortgage back (which is registered), with or without interest, usually without periodic payments, which is due in three, five, seven, or ten years. Often, the due date is linked to some expected future event, such as the time when the kids should be finished school or are otherwise independent, or when the remaining spouse can be expected to have finished some course for employment upgrading.

2. He or she remains on the title, with the condition that there will be a future payment (at some specified time) for either a portion of the equity which then exists, or a specified sum (which may attract interest in the interim).

Sometimes, these delayed payout options can offer significant benefits to both parties.

If you have come to the conclusion that the house must be sold, you probably need to ask:

- "If we sell the house for X dollars in the next 90 days, how will we share the proceeds?"

- "Can we each carry on or will we be worse off?"

- "Where will we go afterward?"

If you do not know the answer to these questions, you need to consider the options carefully.

Remember, as well, that there can be many advantages or disadvantages to selling, depending on your particular situation. The following are some of the advantages of selling:

- A sale and a move creates a "clean break," and for some parties, that's key. Having a nice fresh start in new premises can be helpful for economic, social, and psychological reasons. Often, a move to a new home can be enlightening and invigorating — maybe even fun!

- A sale can encourage settlement. Sometimes, once the mortgage is cleared and the parties have a little cash on hand, it's easy to explore and recognize options and opportunities. A sale can be a cathartic economic event that will move you both closer to a resolve of all the issues. After all, in many families, the home is the biggest and most valuable asset.

- Sale proceeds (no matter how limited) can provide a tool for equalization of inequities. For instance, if one spouse has a claim to compensatory or lump-sum spousal support and the other has no ability to pay, selling the home can help. Access to the cash that was once equity in the home can help to finance retraining for a spouse.

- Selling the home can force the resolution of other issues. For instance, even though some parties profess that they are positioned and fighting over every issue and can't agree on anything, I rarely hear that from clients when it's time to divide lawn furniture, Christmas decorations, or other incidentals. The fact is that on moving day, separating spouses seem to find a way to resolve their differences over matters that might otherwise seem insurmountable. It's like the energy you discovered as a student the night before your term paper was due. Three weeks earlier, you couldn't imagine working on it, but once your back was against the wall, anything was possible. The pressure of disposing of chattels on moving day is a wonderful persuader.

There are some distinct disadvantages to selling the family home, which include:

- It's disruptive. Selling and moving upsets kids, pets, and just about everything else.

- It's expensive. It costs money to transfer the electricity account, phone, cable, as well as the cost for notifying the post office. You will also end up giving away many thousands of dollars in equity to a realtor (or, worse still, selling for less than market rates if you elect to do it yourself).

- Selling means moving to a new place where the neighbors, schools, house, and just about everything else are unknown. These uncertainties can be challenging, concerning, and in some cases, costly.

- A sale often means prepayment of the mortgage, and perhaps a significant penalty for early discharge of the mortgage.

- A sale may trigger tax.

- Selling your home when there's no settlement means that, in all likelihood, the net proceeds are going to end up in some lawyer's trust account, awaiting resolution. This, of course, is the worst possible destination for sale proceeds for a number of reasons. One is that the lawyers then know that the parties are armed, equipped, and able to battle. Another is that the funds usually earn little or no interest, and being out of the market often means being precluded from building equity. Then, of course, there's always the ultimate reason — you can't live in a lawyer's trust account. Nobody benefits from having money tied up indefinitely.

Note: In my practice, when parties have sold a house but can't decide how to divide the proceeds, I often find that, at the very least, they can agree on a three-way split of the equity (i.e., one third goes to the husband, one third to the wife, and the balance stays in trust pending resolution of the dispute). By this method, both parties get something, and yet there is a safe pool of proceeds reserved for later argument.

While the topic is being pondered, remember that there's rarely anything urgent that needs to be dealt with in respect to the home. Usually, taking a week or two to think about the options isn't a particularly risky proposition, although listing and selling in a panic can be disastrous.

When you think about the options, remember the above, but also consider the following factors:

- Usually, the party in possession of the property pays the mortgage, taxes, and general upkeep. If that person happens to be a mother who is child-rearing and not earning an income, it may be necessary to deal with spousal and child support to make possession possible, but generally speaking, that's ancillary. Typically, courts do not kick the mom and the kids out of the house because dad has the income and can afford to pay the mortgage. A more usual course is to leave the mom and the children in the home and order spousal and child support. When assessing this issue, courts typically decide the case on the basis of which party has the better claim to occupation and possession, and then decide who will pay what. That is the order in which the topics are addressed. The status quo will be a key factor.

- Sometimes, after a sale, the parties will be astonished to find that although they qualified for mortgage financing as a couple inside the marriage neither qualifies for financing after the marriage, and they cannot get back into the market, no matter what the sale produced. That's even more likely now in the aftermath of the 2008 housing meltdown — banks have tighter lending policies and practices, and are often more cautious, particularly with parties who are going through a divorce.

- Occasionally, a sale will cause trouble or create other issues. Once in a while, following a sale, I find that a spouse who has been miserable in a relationship will leave the area and start a new life in a different town, creating all sorts of new mobility, access, and financial issues. Other times, I find that recently separated spouses manage a sale of the home and then quickly enter into new relationships, which invites all sorts of other considerations and issues.

- Sometimes a sale can give parties a once-in-a-lifetime opportunity to establish savings and retirement portfolios. This can often be done with sale proceeds, sometimes with considerable tax savings. Parties who have never been able to put money away for retirement can often manage to do that when the house has been liquidated. Depending on market forces, interest rates, and other variables, this can be a very good thing.

- Occasionally, a sale will actually be very beneficial to spouses who have overextended themselves with consumer credit, or otherwise managed to bind themselves to high interest and oppressive loans. While it's never good to liquidate an equitable asset for short-term gain, if you and your spouse have debts at 11, 15, or 20 percent interest, using home sale proceeds to clear those obligations can produce profound and immediate relief that might not have been imaginable any other way.

The principle here is similar to the point I often raise with clients about refinancing. From time to time, I encounter clients who have racked up consumer credit card debt and rewritten their family mortgage to pay off these obligations. This is often repeated on multiple occasions. The logic behind this is simple on the surface. The refinancing spouses say to themselves: "We were paying 20 percent on the MasterCard, but now we've rewritten our mortgage to pay off the debt, and the mortgage is only at 6 percent, so we've saved a ton of money." That logic, of course, seems appealing, but it has to be remembered that the credit card debt has now been refinanced at a lower rate of interest for an amortization period of 25 years! Interest on a $10,000 debt over 25 years is still oppressive. Refinancing consumer debt in a mortgage only makes sense if the term is short, and the payments are high.

Selling a home to pay debts makes sense, by the same token, but only if there is a commitment to changed behavior after the sale, and a new appreciation that high interest debt must be avoided.

2. Pensions

Nowhere in family law is there more misunderstanding and apprehension than in the area of pensions. As mentioned in Chapter 7, pensions are often undervalued, misunderstood, and overlooked by the parties and even their professional advisors for a number of reasons.

First, pensions aren't very easily understood. They are complex schemes, usually understood by an elite few, and are often described and governed by complicated legislation and contracts. They cannot be sold or traded outside of a family, so not much public effort is made to test their value. Moreover, as alluded to previously, since pensions really consist of two essential elements — a present value as a savings instrument *and* an entitlement to a future stream of periodic payments — they are hard to estimate or value.

The long-term value of a pension clearly distinguishes it from almost every other kind of family asset. For instance, if parties are trying to estimate the worth of their home, they can call an appraiser, a realtor, or do some research themselves. By looking in local newspapers, keeping tabs on recent sales, and spending a few hours on the Internet, most homeowners are able to make a relatively educated guess as to a range for value on their home. It's that way with cars, boats, and other major family assets.

That is not the case, however, in respect to pensions. In fact, misunderstandings over valuing pensions have caused many unfair and improper deals to be brokered.

Parties who don't know the actual worth of a pension (because they have not retained an actuary) may be tempted to simply use a recent contributor statement to find out what the portfolio is worth. This is a dangerous practice that invariably results in the parties being misinformed as to value. As a result, in any case where one party is giving up an interest in a pension or agreeing to take some other asset in exchange, I recommend that an actuary be engaged. If given the opportunity to review the particulars, actuaries are able to give opinions about the present value of a pension by reference to the saved portion of the fund and the terms and conditions of the plan. For the cost of between $500 and $1,500, you can acquire an estimate of value that will serve you well in the years to come. Settling without that is just plain dangerous.

Remember, too, that if you have agreed to share pensions (usually because both spouses have a pension), the actual wording and language of the sharing paragraph can be tricky. Many plans, funds, and administrators take the position that unless the wording of the specific pension division paragraph conforms with their rules, they can refuse to divide the fund (thereby thwarting the legitimate intention of the parties). This can be disastrous. As a result, it's always good policy to ask the plan administrator for a sample division clause. You can sometimes do this by phone, but I usually make the request in writing. It's as simple as Sample 3.

Finally, keep in mind that many pensions have options that are available to the participant/annuitant, which can be selected depending on the mechanics of the plan. For instance, a spouse who has earned an entitlement to participate in a spouse's pension may be able to take a joint survivor option. The joint survivor option usually means that if

SAMPLE 3
Letter to the Fund Administrator

(Date)

(Your address)

To the Fund Administrator:

I am Sally Johnson, the spouse of James Johnson. James and I separated last October, and we wish to divide his pension equally between us. We wonder if you have some specific rules or language which we might incorporate into our separation agreement to effect this.

Also, please advise if there is an administrative fee for making the division.

I thank you in advance for your assistance.

Sincerely,

Sally Johnson
Sally Johnson

---

the annuitant dies and leaves behind a surviving spouse, the spouse is entitled to some benefits, even though the annuitant is gone. Whether the survivor option exists or applies in the case of a separation is something that must be examined in regard to the particulars of the plan in question. Moreover, it will be important to deal with the joint survivor option in the agreement, and how to establish proof that the option has been elected and cannot be revoked.

I cannot possibly offer advice about that here in the absence of specifics, but I can say that you will need to know the answers to these issues *before* you deal with division of the pension. Start with a copy of the pension plan benefits statement, and then ask questions. A call to the fund or plan administrator can be informative. If you do not understand something about a pension, investigate further. Most lawyers are experienced in dealing with pension questions and will know how to get answers for you.

3. Property Transfers

If you and your spouse own property, you will want to divide that property upon separation. When you do, you will very likely need to document the transaction. Sometimes, it's not enough to just say that you intend to transfer the asset. For example, saying that you'll transfer a car or a house in an agreement simply isn't adequate. In most jurisdictions, other documents will be necessary to achieve the objective. The separation agreement should describe the intention, and the ancillary transfer documents will be executed to seal the deal and formalize the transaction.

Throughout most of North America, the ownership of land is recorded in a central registry or government office where deeds and title certificates are kept and recorded. Exactly how this all works varies widely from one area to another.

In my jurisdiction, for instance, we do not use deeds. Instead, we keep track of the ownership of land in a central registry where the ownership of all land is recorded. This is now done electronically. When title to land changes hands, a document must be electronically transmitted or delivered to the registry to record the transaction. There is a small fee for this service. All important charges and encumbrances against property are also recorded in this way. That means that an electronic search of the registry will reveal who owns the property, if there is a mortgage on title to the property, and other charges if there are any (e.g., spousal liens, judgments, tax certificates, and similar claims).

The practice in other areas may vary slightly, but the theory is the same in most places. Accordingly, if you intend to deal with ownership of land in a separation agreement, you will very likely need to deal with a land registry office or government clerk at some point.

That's true, also, with respect to motor vehicles (the ownership of which is usually recorded in a central government office). A system coexists to record the ownership of motorhomes, mobile and modular homes, large boats, motorcycles, and some other types of vehicles. If you and your spouse want to divide your property and there exists a system for the proper registration of land or vehicles, you need to not only state your intentions in your separation agreement — you also need to deal with the central registry and effect compliance with local property laws. Your failure to do so may complicate matters and could lead to confusion and uncertainty later.

If you are agreeing to transfer a car from one spouse to the other, you need to be careful. Say, for instance, that the car has a loan registered against it. If there is consumer financing (i.e., a car loan), it's probably on the title and follows the car even if you transfer it from one spouse to the other. Because the loan is registered against the title to the vehicle and will travel with the vehicle as it moves from one party to the other, there could be trouble if the loan is not paid. Perhaps an example is best:

Joan and John have two trucks (e.g., a Ford and a Dodge). They are both registered in John's name, because John uses them for work and thinks that there's a tax advantage to this. When Joan and John separate, it's agreed that Joan will keep the Ford, and John will have the Dodge. They put that in the agreement, but neglect to do the paperwork necessary to effect the transfers at the Motor Vehicle Registry office in town. Later, Joan defaults on the loan payments, and Ford Credit seizes the truck and sues John (the registered owner) for the deficiency and the costs. Because the vehicle is legally his personal property, he's liable to Ford and will lose the case. His credit rating is now damaged. He can claim against Joan, of course, but she's living in Grand Cayman with another man.

Further complications can arise if the lender on a car loan is not a willing participant to the transaction. For instance:

Tom and Teresa have a Chevy car. The car is registered in Teresa's name. In their separation documents, the parties have agreed that Tom will take the Chevy with him. The car is worth about $10,000, but there is $6,000 owing on it. The equity is $4,000. Tom pays Teresa $2,000 when the car is transferred (to compensate her for the fact that he's getting all the equity in the car and she is giving up her half of the equity). He does that, and then contacts the lender to transfer the loan. The car is financed with ABC Bank. The loan document says that if the parties sell or transfer the vehicle, the bank is entitled to payment of the loan in full. There may even be an interest penalty clause. In any event, when Tom goes to ABC bank to describe the deal, the banker makes the demand. Tom says he'll just take over the loan. The problem arises when ABC says that they're not interested in a new loan with Tom. Because he has a poor credit history and an obligation to pay Teresa support, they demand payment in full and tell Tom to get the money elsewhere. If he doesn't, they say they may have to seize the vehicle. In this circumstance, the parties have made a deal that compromises the rights of a third party (the lender), and have not made the appropriate inquiries in advance.

The worst case scenario can sometimes occur through simple error. Let's say a vehicle is going to be transferred in an agreement, but the documents necessary to facilitate the transfer are forgotten or overlooked. The person who possesses and uses the vehicle is not the registered owner. One day, the insurance lapses and for a few days, there's no coverage. If the driver then rear-ends another motorist, the registered owner (not the driver) can be liable. An even worse scenario is unveiled where the person using the vehicle hits and injures a pedestrian while drunk, and so there's a breach of the insurance policy and no coverage at all. In such circumstances, the registered owner (who may not have any use of the car) can be held liable.

When real estate is transferred, great care must be exercised, because, frankly, the amount of money and the risk involved will be more significant. The process can be tricky because banks and mortgage companies are often even more fussy and particular about security instruments, transfers, and giving releases. Usually, when a mortgage is made for the purchase of a home, the bank wants both spouses named on the mortgage as borrowers. That's because the loan is usually for a relatively large amount of money, and so the bank wants all the security and certainty that's available. Having two borrowers (or obligors) is better than one, and the bank will almost invariably want a promise of repayment from both parties. When the couple separates, the bank may be unwillingly to release one of the borrowers unless there's good reason for so doing. As a result, if spouses intend to transfer property which is encumbered by a registered line of credit or mortgage, it's important to know what position the bank is going to take *before* the deal is done. Work with the bank, and you'll likely be able to satisfactorily resolve the issue. Sometimes, the best agreeable solution is to replace the departing spouse with a guarantor. Other times, the bank will simply rewrite the mortgage with the remaining spouse. The bank is unlikely to be willing to do this, unless there's a higher interest rate to be payable on the new mortgage. Because of the intricacies of these transactions, you may need to engage a lawyer or broker to assist you for this purpose.

Remember that if you are planning to transfer the home from both spouses to one spouse, or from one spouse to the other, you will need to give notice to the bank or mortgage company. Failure to do so may constitute a breach of your loan agreement, and may entitle the bank or mortgage company to take action against you. In some circumstances, you may unknowingly trigger a foreclosure, even if the payments are current. Again, the laws about these matters are quite different from place to place, so proceed with caution.

Remember, as well, that your willingness to leave your spouse with the liability and responsibility for the loan or mortgage does not necessarily mean that the lender will be like-minded. That's particularly true in the aftermath of the 2008 meltdown. Be prepared to deal with this possibility if and when it arises. What will you do if the mortgage company will not give you or your spouse a release? Will you be willing to transfer the equity away notwithstanding? Will your continued exposure or liability for this mortgage imperil your ability to borrow if you later want to buy another house and need another loan or mortgage? What if you make the deal, remain liable, and your spouse defaults on the mortgage? Will you be willing to pick up the pieces? Obviously, that may be less of a worry if there's significant equity in the property, but given what has happened in the mortgage and housing market in the last few years, we now all know that anything can happen.

If you are going to transfer significant property such as a car or a house, you need to think about two things:

1. Is there a registry or other central government office where the transfer must be recorded?

2. Are there loans or other encumbrances or interests that will be affected by the transaction?

Considering these questions in advance will reduce the likelihood of surprise or disappointment later.

4. Family Business or Company

When separating spouses own a legal interest in a company or business, special care must be taken to ensure that the entity is dealt with properly. If the interests of the parties in the company are not dealt with correctly and as part of an overall settlement, the spouses may unwittingly continue to share their interest for many years to come. That may not be any great inconvenience if the business is, for instance, the husband's small electrical company, which is stable and successful. However, what if the husband makes a mistake at work, is uninsured, and the construction project he's working on burns to the ground? Would the wife from whom he separated five years ago be liable for damages? The answer is perhaps.

For these and many other reasons, it's important to deal with business and company interests once and for all in an agreement, just as you'd deal with a car, a credit card, or some other asset or liability.

There are several ways in which families can be involved in a business venture:

- One or both of the parties own shares in an incorporated company.

- One or both of the parties own, operate, manage, or work in a business which is not incorporated, but has value, and in which they have an interest either as borrowers or as legal or equitable owners. This usually arises when one spouse works in a partnership, as a sole proprietor, or in some other entrepreneurial venture or business relationship.

- One of the spouses is a participant in a joint venture or other business activity, and it can be argued that by reason of the spousal relationship, there is a shared liability or responsibility.

- One of the spouses is a partner in a partnership.

The law about business relations and incorporations is complex, and varies from state to state and from province to province. As a general rule, if one of the separating spouses has a business interest which has value or may attract a liability or responsibility, legal advice about the separation will be necessary. Maybe the non-owning spouse has financial obligations as the spouse of a shareholder or partner. Maybe the non-owning spouse has signed corporate documents, guarantees, or other commitments which bind him or her to certain responsibilities. Or perhaps the fact of the separation itself is inadequate to insulate the non-owning spouse from the prospect of liability if the company, partnership, or business commits an act of negligence, breaches a law, or becomes a defendant in some new action. It's simply too difficult to know about these risks without legal representation.

The risk of complication and liability is too big to be ignored. Get counsel, and ask for disclosure. In many circumstances, the method for protecting a spouse in such circumstances can be easily accommodated.

If corporate assets must be disposed of in a separation, there will also be significant tax issues to address. When one spouse disposes of a corporate or business interest, tax can be triggered. Sometimes the amount of tax can be onerous, particularly if the disposition comes to the taxpayer as a personal gain. Again, when disposing of a family business or interest in a family business, get advice and proceed with caution.

4.1 Valuation and compensation of a business interest

Similarly troublesome can be valuation and compensation issues. Simply stated, if you are leaving a relationship in which a business interest is an asset, you may be entitled to compensation. Finding out what your interest is worth can be a little tricky, and may require an opinion from a business valuator, chartered accountant, or other professional. Do not walk away from a business interest without that advice, no matter how simple the business may seem.

Most family law lawyers will know the professionals in the area who can assist with valuation matters. In a simple case, the estimate of value can often be obtained simply and inexpensively, particularly if the business is small, new, or a franchise operation with many comparables. However, if you are leaving a long-term relationship in which your spouse has operated a valuable business that has produced a steady stream of income, be wary. The compensation to which you may be entitled is likely not easily estimated by a lawyer during a one-hour consultation. Frankly, if you are leaving a valuable corporate entity behind, expect to spend some money to establish your right to compensation. You really need to have an expert valuation.

I once acted for a professional who had a significant interest in a medical facility. My client was the husband, and he wanted me to argue several things. One of the points he wanted me to make was that while he was prepared to pay his wife squarely and fairly for her half interest in the business, he was going to need to borrow the money to do so. He'd be making payments on that, including interest, and he wanted that fact remembered when the spousal support topic was considered. His capacity to pay spousal support would be compromised in the reality of his post-separation world, due to the loan he would be repaying.

Second, he did not agree with the valuation that the wife's accountant had offered. He thought that the wife's expert had been unduly optimistic about some projections, had overlooked several negative contingencies, and had incorrectly assumed some tax facts. We needed to have our own expert reply.

I hired the best expert I knew and provided all the materials. The process was complicated because there were several interconnected companies, funding and debt issues, and other shareholders who were reluctant to share information.

At the end of it all, I got the expert opinion I had hoped for, but it came at a cost of $15,000. My client was horrified with that expense until the court judgment was revealed, and he learned that we had reduced more than $100,000 from the wife's expert valuation. Had we not undertaken that expert expense, it is very doubtful that we could have proven the matters necessary to succeed on those points in court. My client would have overpaid for the interest in the companies which he preserved, and would have been saddled with an unmanageable debt *plus* ongoing spousal support.

5. Resolve Liability Issues

When separating spouses have debt, it's necessary to resolve issues about liability (or legal responsibility) for these debts. If you and your spouse do not settle this issue as part of a comprehensive resolve, the topic can easily come back to haunt you later. If the debt is a $2,500 credit card obligation, the trouble may be nothing more than an inconvenience; however, if the matter involves a corporate line of credit, a mortgage, or a business loan, the consequences can be disastrous.

The first step is to clearly identify the issue. To use a hypothetical, let's assume that Ted and Terry are separating. They have three debts. One is a credit card, one is a car loan, and the other is a joint line of credit. The first step toward handling the issue squarely is to identify the debts.

To do that, the parties must list all the debts. As mentioned in Chapter 6, making a list of assets and liabilities is a good place to begin. There is no magic to the document itself — as long as the items are identified in a sensible way, the purpose will be served.

These debts would be listed with some particularity, as follows:

1. Washington Mutual Visa card (in the name of Ted and Terry, jointly), with balance owing of $3,900 as at June 1, 2011.

2. Clearwater Credit car loan (in Ted's name alone) secured against Ted's 2009 Toyota Truck, with balance owing of $19,000 as at June 1, 2011.

3. Canacash line of credit (in the name of Ted and Terry, jointly) with a balance owing of $4,500, and a credit limit of $10,000, as at June 1, 2011.

This description is adequate for the purposes of our example. Note that approximate balances are adequate. Exact figures are better, but this will do for the purposes of this exercise. Note, too, that some care has been taken to correctly identify the party who is responsible for the debt.

Now let's say that in our example, Ted is willing to take on the Washington Mutual Visa card and the Toyota loan, as long as Terry takes over the line of credit. That would make sense on a "rough justice" basis if Ted is keeping possession of the Toyota vehicle, since it divides responsibility approximately equally.

To achieve this result, the following paragraphs (in the body of the agreement) might be appropriate:

In respect to the three debts listed above Ted and Terry agree that:

- *Ted shall take sole and exclusive liability and responsibility for the Washington Mutual Visa card and the Clearwater Credit loan (since he is keeping possession of the Toyota) and shall at all times hereafter indemnify and save harmless Terry of and from any and all liability in respect thereto.*

- *Terry shall take sole and exclusive liability and responsibility for the Canacash line of credit and shall, at all times hereafter, indemnify and save harmless Ted of and from any and all liability in respect thereto.*

That, on the surface, appears to resolve the matter.

The trouble with all this, of course, is that Washington Mutual and Canacash are not parties to the agreement, and so cannot be held to it, or bound by it. If Ted fails to honor his commitment, Terry cannot very well expect any sympathy at Washington Mutual. They do not care what Ted and Terry agreed to. Their objective will be to collect the debt from the easiest target, and leave the dispute as to contribution and indemnity up to Ted and Terry.

The same is true with respect to the Canacash line of credit. If Terry racks up the line of credit to the maximum and then moves to the Cook Islands, Ted will be left with the debt. He may be able to sue

Terry for breach of the agreement, but that won't help much if Cana-cash sues and obtains judgment, and then seizes Ted's assets.

With regard to the truck loan, of course, the situation is slightly different for at least two reasons. First, the loan is in Ted's name alone, and so Terry cannot be sued on that loan. If Ted fails to pay, the lender may sue or seize the truck, but the lender will not be able to make Terry pay. Second, there is some equity in the truck and, presumably, the loan is registered by the lender against the truck. Ted cannot dispose of the truck without paying off the loan (unless he tricks a purchaser into buying it). If he breaches, he'll lose the truck, but it won't be Terry's problem.

The net effect of all this is that if there is any reason for any dis-trust whatsoever, other arrangements should be made. The best and cleanest approach is to pay the debts in full at the time of separation, and obtain releases from the lender. Both spouses can obtain a copy of the release and know that they are free and clear of that respon-sibility. In the case of a line of credit, make sure that the account is closed so that the line is not re-advanceable after the fact.

If you and your spouse decide that a debt is to be assumed (i.e., taken on) by one spouse to the exclusion of the other, you'll need clear language to explain that. Explain what the debt is, what the terms are, and then make sure that the third party knows. In this way, you can expect to avoid future trouble if something goes wrong.

9

Negotiating Who Gets What

When you and your spouse separate, it may be desirable and indeed necessary to talk about the reasons for the breakdown in the relationship, the circumstances that led up to the separation, and other personal and psychosocial topics. These may all constitute legitimate issues that are deserving of discussion. Unfortunately, I can offer no advice about these topics, and nothing contained in this book is likely to assist parties in their personal relationship issues.

Discussions about adultery, compromised integrity, bad behavior, and other contentious topics should be specifically avoided when the "business side" of the separation is under consideration. Hopefully, you can put these issues away prior to the commencement of negotiations.

If you and your spouse have not and cannot overcome hurt feelings, hostilities, and other insecurities or pains, it is probably going to be difficult to calmly negotiate about the house and credit cards. Hurt feelings can easily affect and destroy conversations, but must not be permitted to influence your discussions or decisions about custody, access, support, and property division. Obviously, that's advice that's easy to dispense and hard to enforce. Many motivated and committed parents cannot solve their family law issues because they have not recovered from the hurt of marriage breakdown.

If you and your spouse have not explored your personal relationship issues before you approach the business side of the separation, it is unlikely that your initial negotiations will be productive unless you agree to put those problems aside. Some couples can separate their relationship pains from their business issues, but it's not easy. Getting past the hurt in order to do business is critical, and sometimes only accomplished with the assistance of counsel, a mediator, or a psychologist.

The purpose here is to assist couples in the process of negotiating (in a peaceful way) toward a satisfactory separation. Part of that process involves a commitment by the parties to leave the emotional baggage on the doorstep to the negotiation room, and earnestly engaging in an honest and genuine way to a concessionary process. Really, that's easier than it sounds, and one of the keys is to remember that you must walk before you run. Keeping a clinical or businesslike approach to the issues will help.

Negotiating a sensible separation agreement is something best done in stages or on a piecemeal basis. By that, I don't mean that the discussions must continue over many painful months or result inevitably in a 50-page written contract. Rather, I suggest that parties focus on easy topics in the beginning, build momentum in the negotiation process, and capitalize on partial successes and resolutions while developing a cooperative pattern. It's really all about taking small, cautious steps in the process before running off to the finish line.

Perhaps an example can best illustrate this point about getting down to business in a measured and metered way:

Assume that at the end of Sue and Sam's traditional, long-term marriage, they meet to negotiate a settlement. Sue is hurt by Sam's infidelity, but agrees to put that aside for the time being. She's anxious to make a deal which is survivable and will give her enough money to support herself and the kids. She hopes to keep the house.

Sam is also eager to move on, and is willing to pay proper support. He's worried, however, that Sue's angry demands will leave him penniless, and he's anxious to ensure that he maintains a proper home so he can have the children over regularly.

If Sam and Sue put all the cards on the table in the first 15 minutes, it's very likely that they will fail in their attempts to negotiate. Sam will set out his ultimate objective and Sue will feel threatened. She'll conclude that, once again, Sam is being selfish, and that his demands fail to take into consideration the considerable mess that he's made for her and the kids. Soon, the discussion will deteriorate, the issue of Sam's sexual transgressions will arise, and the session will end with ongoing distrust and unhappiness.

If, however, the parties focus on the easy topics first, they may be able to build momentum and recapture some element of trust. In our hypothetical, that might mean settling non-contentious issues (and recording those points) during the first meeting. For instance, it may be assumed and obvious that Sam will keep the truck and Sue will keep the van. This is unlikely to be a contentious topic, so the parties should record their agreement on that point, and if necessary, complete the vehicle registration transfers to finalize that part of the arrangement. Doing so takes one topic off the table and reassures the parties that they can solve some things. This can be a building block and will help to establish a cooperative atmosphere.

When I am negotiating with counsel in similar circumstances, I sometimes hear lawyers say that they won't deal piecemeal, and they want an all-or-nothing deal. I understand the logic of this. In some toxic breakups, it's best to wrap up the arrangement in one swoop, and have each and every term agreed to concurrently and in writing because the level of distrust and the acrimony is so pronounced. Usually, however, that's not the case, particularly so when litigation is not pending.

When separating spouses are trying to resolve their issues at home, without counsel or litigation, there's a different atmosphere and a different feel to the discussion. In our example above, when Sam agrees to keep the truck and Sue agrees to keep the van, neither spouse is conceding anything about value. The deal for ownership settles title only — it says nothing about whether Sue owes Sam or Sam owes Sue. In our hypothetical, we haven't come to that point yet. Maybe it won't be an issue. Or, perhaps, because one vehicle is of greater value, there will have to be a separate compensatory payment. That can and should be discussed.

As the process of negotiation wears on (over several minutes, several hours, several days, or perhaps even weeks), you should make notes about these partial victories and interim successes. This can help to build momentum and trust.

Some of the easy topics include possession and ownership of cars, furnishings, and other household items, child access or visitation, including shared parenting arrangements for Father's Day or Mother's Day, birthdays, religious holidays, and summer vacations, and guardianship. In the vast majority of cases, parents with even a modicum of devotion to the process can overcome disputes on these topics. Working out these incidentals early on can be very useful.

Great lawsuits (and movies) have developed around custodial issues (remember the fictitious *Kramer vs. Kramer* film) and even possession of the family home (e.g., *The War of the Roses*). The fact is that reasonable people can easily behave unreasonably and fight over anything if permitted or encouraged to do so. What's likely to be an inconsequential and simple starting point for one couple may be the most acrimonious issue for another.

1. Dividing the Small Household Items

One tip I have for parties who are working on a momentum-building agreement is to start with a schedule to divide household items that are typically inconsequential. Even though I recall that some great battles have ensued over antiques, mementos, photographs, and other keepsakes, the value of such items rarely justifies a hard-fought dispute over ownership.

If the parties can resolve some or all of these topics, they should record their successes in writing (initially without any consideration of value or the monetary worth of the assets). Later, values can be assigned to the items, and one party may be asked to pay the other some compensation.

In saying this, however, there are a few key points to keep in mind:

- Almost nothing that any "normal" family owns is worth a great lawsuit. Unless you possess the Hope Diamond, a Rembrandt painting, or several Ferrari cars, it's probably best to be fair and compromising, and move on to an agreement as swiftly as possible. Don't be a doormat, but don't get into litigation over a parrot and a deep freeze. Nothing that we regular folk own is worth a bloodbath.

- Almost anything that you own can be valued and compensated. If you are absolutely convinced that the asset division is grossly unfair, consider whether it's worth talking about a compensation payment to level the division.

- An *in specie* division (keeping assets in their present form rather than selling) is probably better than a lopsided division that requires an offsetting payment. Separating parties are almost always short of cash, so taking a better BBQ instead of a check may be easier and more sensible.

- Don't fight over kids' stuff. The bedroom furnishings, toys, and other household items that belong to the kids should stay or go with the kids, depending on principal or primary residency. That means that the parent with primary residency should keep the lion's share of the children's chattels. If parenting is truly shared on a nearly equal basis, the children's stuff will have to be divided relatively evenly, so that neither party suffers hardship. Try to solve this early on, so that the kids feel comfortable in both homes.

- If you can't settle on the division of household contents, there are only a few solutions. All the alternatives are less desirable than a consensual division. Keep in mind that litigation is not an alternative with respect to household items. Judges will generally not entertain argument over furnishings and effects, and if the parties cannot settle the issue, there will be a lottery, an auction, or a forced sale. In such circumstances, both parties lose. The following alternatives may help with your division of small assets:

  - One alternative worth consideration is the two-list process. By this method, one party (selected by the toss of a coin) prepares two lists. He or she theoretically puts one half of the household items on the A list, and one half of the contents on the B list. The other party (who had no hand in drawing the list) then chooses either list A or list B. The party who prepares the list will be careful to fairly divide the contents evenly between list A and list B because the list maker will have no idea which list will be selected. This ensures that the lists are not lopsided and are balanced. Further, any item that is overlooked or not included by the list maker automatically passes to the chooser. This ensures that the lists are complete.

• Another alternative is to have all the household contents appraised by a chosen and impartial property appraiser. At that point, a judge, a mediator, or an arbitrator can hear from the parties and make a decision as to who gets what, and then a compensation payment is made by the party who received the more valuable assets. This method almost certainly ensures that nobody is happy, but it does resolve the dispute.

• Another method is to prepare a comprehensive inventory of household items. With the toss of a coin, one party proceeds first. Party One makes a selection, and then it's time for Party Two to make a choice. This process continues until all the chattels have been divided. At the end, it may or may not be necessary to have a compensatory payment made.

Remember that it may be helpful to consider whether, as the assets are being divided, there should be discussion about fair market value, or replacement value. Depending on the circumstances of the parties, the cash on hand, the overall asset position, and needs, a division that's based on fair market value may leave one spouse in a very difficult economic position.

2. What to Do When You Come Across Obstacles in the Negotiation Process

From time to time, you and your spouse will hit roadblocks in the negotiation process. These obstacles or stalemates may occur periodically, or whenever you come to a particularly tricky topic. Sometimes, your inability to overcome one of these obstacles will stall the entire process.

Relax! It's normal to have good and bad days in the negotiation process. Having a bad session, a difficult topic, or becoming bogged down at a certain point in the process does not mean that all hope is lost or that you'll never be able to resolve the issues.

The following list includes some of the steps and techniques that can be utilized to help get the discussions back on track. There are many other ideas which can be employed, but here are a few for consideration:

- If you become deadlocked on one particular topic or issue, skip it. Leave the tough concept aside for the time being, and move on to something else. In most separation scenarios, there are many issues to canvass. If you're stalled, talk about other things and see if you can build momentum there. You may be able to successfully return to the hard topics later.

- Sometimes, writing down the past or partial successes (which you have already settled) can be inspirational. For instance, if you have managed to resolve three or four money topics, but are encountering difficulty figuring out how to share parenting responsibilities, take an hour or a day or a week to record the consensus, and then agree to meet afterward to talk about parenting, after you've recorded the consent. By this method, you not only put off the tough issue, you also tend to build confidence and calm by recognizing past success. Believe it or not, confirming an agreement (even a partial agreement) can be rewarding and helpful.

- Agree to disagree on the few truly contentious topics, and deal with them through a mediator, a judge, an arbitrator, a counselor, or another method.

- Ask yourself if it's really necessary to reach a decision on the sensitive topic at the present time. Sometimes, talking about long-term solutions to enduring problems can become less onerous if the parties understand that it's not critical to find a resolution instantly. For instance, I find that while separating spouses can often agree that spousal support is needed, affordable, and payable, they become absolutely stalemated when it comes time to talk about duration. By that I mean that although the parties agree that one spouse shall pay the other spouse $1,000 a month, they disagree about how long the payments should continue. In such circumstances, it may not be necessary to find a solution to that question instantly. Both parties know that the sum is needed and payable now. Both agree that it's going to continue for two to five years. If there's no consensus on duration, perhaps it's best to continue the payments for one year, and then agree to meet again at that time and talk further. If there is still no solution, other options (e.g., arbitration, mediation) will still be available. Besides, sometimes circumstances will change in the interim. New jobs, new relationships, and economic variables will occasionally make the topic less contentious or the proper result more obvious.

- Consider whether there is an alternate way to think about and negotiate the topic. For example, if the deadlock concerns the division of family assets, ask if there's a different approach that might work. Could the division of assets favor the husband if the wife received more spousal support? Or what if the wife gave up her claim for spousal support, and in return received the guest cottage she so desperately wants? Often, deadlocked issues aren't true barriers to settlement; they are simply speed bumps or obstacles. There's almost always a way around a tricky issue if the parties are willing to be creative and flexible in their approach. Again, the fact that the parties themselves cannot imagine a solution does not mean that no solution exists; sometimes what's needed is a fresh approach or an imaginative perspective. Occasionally, an outsider can offer the insight and intuition that's needed to resolve matters.

- Finally, if you have stalled on a particular topic (one that's truly contentious and possibly a dealbreaker), reconsider your overall objectives. Sometimes an impossible or insurmountable dispute really doesn't matter much and isn't worth fighting over. Consider giving up your position as a concession. Perhaps it's best to go to the spouse and say, "Look, we've solved most of our difficulties and I'm grateful to you for your cooperation so far. You know that we disagree on this topic, and there does not appear to be any way to solve the dispute. Rather than risk upsetting a comprehensive settlement, I'm prepared to reconsider. I'll agree to your demand if you're prepared to sign something now to conclude everything." While giving up doesn't seem like much of a negotiation topic, reassessing objectives with a view to concession can be worthwhile, particularly if it means that everything's done. This proposition, of course, is something that can only work effectively if the parties truly are on the cusp of resolution. It may bring into consideration the old adage: You can be right, or you can be happy.

3. Conduct and Other Allegations

When couples separate, it is not uncommon for one or both spouses to feel the need to allocate blame. They do this, I believe, in an attempt to prove to their friends and family members that ending the relationship was fair and proper. They want to be accepted and appreciated, and they want the approval of their friends — particularly those friends who will remain friends after the separation.

It is for that reason that many separating spouses attempt to justify the decision by including in the divorce process allegations that the other spouse is an unfit parent, a slob, a drunk, unfaithful, lazy, and so on. It seems that any allegation at all can be included as a ground or basis for leaving the relationship, so long as it stands a chance of being believed.

In some jurisdictions, when one spouse leaves the relationship, it is necessary to give grounds for the separation. For example, a litigant may need to prove cruelty or adultery to qualify for a divorce. Sometimes, it is simply enough to allege that the relationship is irretrievably broken and that's that. In my jurisdiction, the most common ground that is offered is that the parties have been separate and apart for one year. We call this "no fault" divorce. Really, it probably should not matter why parties have chosen to end their marriage; if it's over, it's over. The government cannot force happy wedlock on anyone, so why pretend? Still, some jurisdictions require one of the spouses to prove fault and so remnants of this concept remain on the books and in the minds of separating spouses.

You don't have this problem, of course, if you were never married. As a common-law spouse, you can wander in and out of marriage-like relationships without needing to prove fault, adultery, or any other reason for the separation. The reason just doesn't matter.

In any event, whether you are leaving a common-law relationship, or living in an "enlightened" state or province in which the reason for the breakup of the marriage is irrelevant, there are some rules about bringing grounds and conduct issues into the fray. These are not rules of court — the following are my observations about what works if you want to experience an amicable separation.

If you are going to allege some aspect or element of bad conduct (whether in your paperwork, in your discussions and negotiations, or as a fact which figures in the separation agreement), make sure you can prove it. You may not need to prove it immediately, but a wild, unfounded, and baseless allegation that cannot be proven will inevitably fuel hostility and acrimony and do nothing to move the matter toward resolution. If you cannot prove a worry, concern, or suspicion, don't allege it. Remember that as soon as you make an allegation that your spouse has bad behavior, habits, or issues, you are very likely to receive a retaliatory complaint. Think carefully about the principle which applies to people who live in glass houses.

If you are going to allege some kind of harmful behavior, make sure that it matters and is relevant. If you dislike your spouse because he or she is messy, disrespectful, and always late, put it aside. Nothing about personality flaws or behavioral defects needs to be included as part of the separation and divorce negotiation process. It just doesn't matter. You are leaving, and that's that. If you were still in love and wanted the relationship to endure, you would probably be able to overlook these little issues (you might even describe them as cute quirks or character traits), but for now, just put them aside. They will bring you nothing.

However, if the reason for the separation really does matter (e.g., a gambling addiction, alcoholism, drug abuse, or some other problem), ask yourself if it's necessary to talk about it. If you cannot live with your spouse because he goes to the casino every other night and can't be trusted with milk money, you probably don't need to mention that anywhere in the paperwork unless it bears on some ongoing issue such as child care. Most probably, it just doesn't matter. You and your spouse both know about the issue. His gambling problem likely does not disqualify him from access to a teenager, although it may mean that he should not have custody and you will need security for support and maintenance.

If the issue is alcohol abuse, that may very well affect your decision and negotiation about the care of a youngster, driving issues, and other matters affecting health and welfare. You might as well deal with it up front. There's no point is pretending that all's well if your spouse can't be trusted to pick up the kids from school once a week or organize a sleep over. Indeed, if you are dealing with drugs, booze, safety, or other welfare issues, it may be tough to negotiate a compromise settlement on children's issues without professional help, although that doesn't mean you cannot settle property and support topics.

I would guess that infidelity is still one of the predominant reasons for matrimonial discord. Although I am aware that there are a few states where infidelity is a ground for divorce (it must be proven), it almost invariably does not matter as far as the negotiated settlement is concerned. Try to keep this in mind. A lascivious spouse does not, by reason of that fact, get less property. The spouse who "fooled around" is not disentitled to support. Because sexual misconduct doesn't matter, don't make it a focus of the discussion. It will not enhance the likelihood of resolution. Besides, you both know what happened. If I had a dollar for every time I had explained this point, I probably wouldn't have to work anymore. Even though this fact is now truly notorious, I still have to explain the principle about once a week in my practice.

I think there must be an explanation for this. Maybe it's that nothing can hurt as much as the breach of trust that comes with adultery. Maybe it's the personal insult from knowing that your lover has been with another person, or prefers that other person. Perhaps it is the sting that comes from the expectation that everyone will know. I don't know much about that, but I do know that spousal misconduct does not matter when negotiating a separation, and should not matter, unless it bears on or affects an issue respecting the care of children. Keep that in mind.

Having said all this, there is something to be said for intelligent action, considerate behavior, decorum, and manners. If you have recently ended a spousal relationship, and are trying to negotiate a compromise agreement and pave the way to a happy new life, use a little common sense. Although you are not prohibited from having a new lover, new interests, or a renewed lustiness, avoid being obvious and stupid about it. Don't slap tongues with your lover in open view of your teenage children. Do not buy your latest lover a new car, and then show up in it. I know it sounds ridiculous that I need to mention these things, but believe me, I draw from experience here.

4. Signing the Agreement

When you have reached a suitable written agreement with your spouse, it should be carefully and legibly recorded. For obvious reasons, the agreement should be typed (not handwritten). A handwritten agreement is probably enforceable if it's legible, but on this continent, in this age, there's no reason to take a chance. Believe it or not, I once defended a lawsuit in which the parties had made a handwritten agreement *in pencil*, and issues about intention, language, and enforcement raged. The bottom line here is that if you have taken the time and effort necessary to make a deal, type it and carefully proof it before it is signed. It will help you to stay out of court.

Ensure that the agreement uses plain language, is clear and understandable, and makes sense. If you have those ingredients in your carefully considered and written agreement, then you have a contract that is ready to be signed.

While the technical rules about signing a legally binding document vary slightly from one jurisdiction to another, there are some fairly universal principles that govern, and they are discussed in the following sections.

4.1 Parties of the agreement

The parties to the contract must sign the contract. If you have a deal that contemplates a settlement between John and Mary Smith, John and Mary must sign — not John and Mary's friend or Mary's sister or Mary's neighbor. This point sounds so obvious that it's hard to imagine that there could ever be any misunderstanding about it, but there often is.

Some examples in which errors occur would include the following:

- John and Mary agree that John is going to transfer the leased car to Mary, but they overlook the fact that they do not own the car. The leasing company does, and so the spouses cannot transfer it. Since the leasing company does not consent to the transfer and is not a party to the agreement, there's a problem here as discussed in Chapter 8.

- John and Mary agree that she'll keep the house and take over the mortgage, but after the fact, the bank does not agree and says Mary does not qualify and the bank won't release John. Since the bank isn't party to the agreement, it's a stalemate.

- John and Mary agree that John's interest in the lakeside cottage is going to be transferred to Mary, but the trustees who own the cottage are not party to the agreement, didn't sign, and won't agree. The transfer cannot be done, and so John and Mary are forced back to the bargaining table.

- John and Mary agree that John's brother will complete the renovations to the den, but John's brother isn't a party, does not agree, and is not bound by the agreement.

4.2 The parties must be competent to sign the agreement

The parties must be capable of contracting. They must be adults (usually 19 years of age), sober, and competent. A drunken, stoned, or otherwise incapable party lacks the basic ability to enter into a binding agreement.

Sometimes, however, the issue of capacity is troublesome but less obvious. For instance, a spouse who has been beaten, threatened, intimidated, or otherwise coerced into a contract likely lacks capacity and cannot be bound by the deal. The intimidation or coercion may, in some circumstances, be quite indirect and mild, yet if it exists to such an extent as to constitute pressure or inducement, the contract may not be enforceable. As a result, it is important for the contracting parties to make their arrangements in the cold, clear light of day, with eyes wide open, and when both parties are competent, sober, and free of pressure and intimidation. If there is anything less than almost perfect freedom in the making of the contract, it is quite likely that one (or both) parties will be able to challenge the contract later.

4.3 Sign the agreement in front of two witnesses

The agreement must be signed by the parties in front of two witnesses. There are a few exceptions to this rule, but they are so limited and unusual that they do not bear mention here.

The question then becomes, who constitutes a witness? The witnesses, like the parties, must be sober, competent adults, and they should not be parties to the agreement. The witnesses must be able to say that they saw you sign the agreement, and all was well. The agreement was read over in the presence of the witnesses. Nobody smelled of booze. Nobody was crying. There were no firearms in the room, and so on.

It's best to have two witnesses, not one. Use one adult, competent, sober witness for one spouse's signature, and another witness for the signature of the other spouse. In the world in which we live, this is no great inconvenience.

The witnesses should be independent and unrelated persons. Do not use family members, best friends, or partisan pals. Your next-door neighbor, acquaintance, grocer, dentist, or realtor are all fine. A notary, lawyer, or other professional can serve as a witness too, although those persons usually charge a fee for the service.

Get a witness who can be found later if there's a dispute. In other words, avoid having a 90-year-old witness. Don't get the kid who works at the corner store or the hitchhiker at the off-ramp on I-5. You may need this witness later. Get someone you can locate if need be.

Have the witness sign after you have signed, and have the witness add his or her current address, phone number, and driver's license number, Social Security Number, or Social Insurance Number as well. This will assist in later identification and location should it be necessary.

10
The Divorce

In most jurisdictions, once the terms of separation have been settled and reduced to a written separation agreement, it's relatively easy, speedy, and inexpensive to process the divorce.

The process and practice for obtaining the divorce varies throughout North America. Fortunately, it is a topic about which there's much information. You may want to start your inquiries on the Internet or by making an appointment for a free consultation with a local lawyer. Do-it-yourself and online divorce kits are available too, and these can be economical and simple. Be wary about general advice and information that is not sensitive to your particular state, province, or territory. (See Self-Counsel Press' website for a divorce kit for your area.)

Obtaining the divorce itself may not require the assistance of a lawyer, but it's always wise to be cautious and make inquiries before proceeding. In some jurisdictions, legal help in processing a divorce is virtually mandatory, given the forms and process that must be meticulously followed. Elsewhere, legal help is entirely optional, although many people are more comfortable having a professional handle the matter.

Remember that you will be pursuing the divorce mainly to free yourself of the former bonds of matrimony — there are actually not many other reasons for getting a divorce order. It's important to keep that in mind. You can probably live separate and apart, peacefully, forever, governed only by a separation agreement. So long as you never try to remarry, the divorce is not really necessary if you have a proper and comprehensive separation agreement. This is a concept often misunderstood. Many people rush to get a quick divorce — sometimes at great expense, often sacrificing important assets and legal principles in the process — thinking that the divorce is what really matters. In fact, it's the reverse; the separation agreement is what matters, and the divorce is the window dressing. The spouse who absolutely must be divorced is the spouse who wishes to remarry. For almost everyone else, it's really optional. That's an important point to remember when you're considering the priorities.

1. The Necessity of Legal Advice When It Comes Time to Divorce

There are several reasons why legal advice about the divorce should be obtained beforehand. For example, in some jurisdictions, certain tax rules exist and apply during the marriage, but cease to exist after divorce. Principles about the tax-exempt status of transferred property, pension division, and other matters can be complex and confusing. It is important to understand these rules and how they may apply to your case before you process the divorce. The tax advantages may vanish with the order for divorce, and you may unwittingly expose yourself to significant costs, penalties, and interest. Talk to a lawyer or an accountant before processing the divorce order.

Although the separation agreement itself is, for most couples, a far more important document, a divorce signifies and finalizes the absolute end of the marriage. It is the divorce that permits remarriage, and forever terminates the legal bond between you and your spouse. As a result, it is important to ensure before processing the divorce that your other legal relations with your spouse have been correctly and completely concluded. If you have not settled pension issues and have not dealt with survivor options, it may be that processing the divorce prematurely can foreclose these options; it may forever preclude your participation in benefits that were available *in* the marriage.

Similarly, if your spouse is about to inherit monies, collect on a personal injury judgment (where injury arose during the currency of the marriage), or is expecting a retroactive tax refund, disability readjustment, or other bonus or compensation, you may want to hold off on the divorce for a while. In some jurisdictions, processing the divorce can preclude your participation in a benefit that might otherwise be available. Again, these rules vary from one jurisdiction to another. They are circumstances that don't arise in the majority of divorce cases, but still, it's better to be safe than sorry. Talk to a lawyer or an accountant before you process the divorce.

Perhaps you're in a rush. Maybe your new partner is pregnant so you are very anxious to marry swiftly. More importantly, if you are in very poor health, facing surgery, a trip to a dangerous country, or some other peril, obtaining the divorce quickly may be important to you. In some jurisdictions, doing so means that the former spouse is thereafter forever precluded from testamentary relief and cannot challenge your will or estate plan. In such circumstances, getting advice about the divorce and proceeding quickly may be important. Give these issues careful thought.

2. Divorce Costs

It's impossible in a book of this type to explain the cost associated with obtaining the divorce order itself. In a jurisdiction which encourages do-it-yourself divorces, the costs can be minimal. In many Canadian jurisdictions, for instance, it's quite possible to process the divorce without counsel for less than $500. However, a lawyer-assisted divorce can cost $1,000 to $2,000 in those same jurisdictions. Whether a lawyer is needed, desired, or advised is something worth investigating. Again, take advantage of free consultations when you can. Many courthouse registries and government offices will provide helpful advice, brochures, and other information about the divorce process, and it's appropriate to learn all you can before you proceed.

If and when you do manage to obtain the divorce order, you will want to keep it with your important papers. Tell you executor, your surviving children, and your best friends where your important papers are kept. Keep the original or a certified copy in your safe deposit box.

In my jurisdiction, divorced spouses can order a large divorce certificate after the process is done. This "suitable for framing" document is slightly more impressive than the marriage certificate which participants received on entering the relationship, and it costs about the same to obtain. I often wonder if there's available data on the comparative costs of entering a marriage (i.e., wedding) versus exiting a marriage (i.e., divorce). One book on divorce, published several years ago, advised readers to plan to spend as much on their divorce as was spent on their wedding! I presume that was included as comic relief.

3. Post-Divorce Problems

It is unfortunately often the case that a troublesome spouse remains troublesome after separation. Every year, a significant number of new files opened in my office deal with enforcement issues. It's sad, but true. Some people simply do not honor the deals they make.

The enforcement issue can arise in a variety of ways. The most typical is a refusal to pay spousal or child support. Another common enforcement problem arises when the access parent doesn't show up for visitation, or refuses to return kids at the end of the session. Less common but equally frustrating problems can occur when one spouse refuses to share information about school, health, or religious activities, or refuses to reveal income changes necessary to determine support quantum.

From time to time, we see chronic cases of this type. I once acted for a mother who was owed more than $100,000 in retroactive child support. On another occasion, I represented a man who had been completely alienated from his children by a mother who refused him access, even though she had agreed on it years earlier.

Many families end up with post-divorce problems. Few can be resolved through negotiation or mediation. Most often, it is necessary to at least threaten legal action before resolution can be found. If that happens in your case, take note of the following principles:

- Threatening to take legal action, or starting legal action to enforce a right or an agreement, does not necessarily mean that you will end up in a trial. Often, all that's needed is the initial threat. It's sometimes the wake-up call that can bring a correction to the situation.

- Delay is bad. If your spouse isn't paying the support to which you are entitled, do something now. Do not wait until the arrears are unmanageable and your children have gone without what was settled upon. A failure to insist and act on your entitlement can look bad and be bad. In some jurisdictions, there is a limitation on how far back the court may go for retroactive correction and collection. Similarly, if there's trouble with access, address it early. Otherwise, it may be suggested that your inaction is evidence that you condoned the complained-of behavior.

- Do not make a compromise without advice. If you are owed $10,000 in back support and agree to take $2,000 cash, make sure you talk with a lawyer first.

- Never, ever, under any circumstances, make a concessionary deal on money in exchange for custody and access compromise. Almost any financial deal that incorporates cash-for-kids principles is likely wholly invalid at law, and may seriously compromise your credibility. Besides, support and access are the rights of a child and cannot be bargained away by a parent.

11

Changing the Agreement

One issue that arises in family law with surprising frequency is the question of how to change a written agreement or court order.

The question arises because circumstances change. Kids grow up. Parents get raises, lose jobs, and acquire assets. Parents who are sharing custody often end up in disputes because there's a new spouse on the horizon, or because an access parent wants to move away. Whatever the reason, you can expect that there may be occasions when the agreement needs review. When it does, there are some rules to remember.

In most jurisdictions, changing an agreement or order is a tricky area of law. It is particularly tricky because the rules that govern changing family law agreements and orders are often very well developed, specific, and vary from one jurisdiction to the next. What's law in one place may be unheard of in another.

In many legal relations, once an agreement or court order has been made, the case is over and the parties go their separate ways. For example, when an injured pedestrian sues a negligent driver for personal injury, he or she obtains a judgment. The insurance company pays the award, and that's the end of the story. Everybody moves on.

It's different, however, with a family law case. That's because as children age, their parenting needs and arrangements change. Maybe the agreement that was made about where the children will live is no longer desirable, practical, or reasonable. These changing circumstances mean that courts and lawmakers have developed rules that are intended to serve two competing interests:

1. First, the law must be certain. There must be reliability and predictability in the rules and principles that govern family law. People who pay support must know with certainty that they cannot simply adjust the payments because "business is slow" for a month. Similarly, the support recipient must understand that it is not possible to apply for an increase just because gas prices increased.

2. Second (and equally important), the law must be elastic enough to ensure that parties who have changed circumstances that are deserving of adjustment or reconsideration are not denied access to justice simply because the system is too inflexible.

Balancing these competing interests is no easy task, and for this reason, it's not uncommon to find an uneven set of rules across the land, describing various schemes and principles intended to serve one concept or the other.

Change can and does arise commonly with respect to support arrangements. Although the agreement that is made for spousal or child support may be fair and proper at the time of separation, changes to the regime may be necessary as children age, parents' jobs change, and incomes increase and decrease. The support plan that is mapped out by cooperative parents of youngsters may genuinely be wholly inadequate for college-bound teens. The spousal support quantum that's settled on in the uncertain aftermath of separation may be grossly unfair two, five, or ten years down the road.

Chances are that in most family law circumstances, there's at least a 50 percent prospect that the agreement or order that's made at the time of separation will need review and change at some point.

Whether the change to be made involves a separation agreement or an order of the court can make a big difference. What document or instrument is to be used to record the change can determine whether or not you need a lawyer.

Here, in point form, are some basic rules to remember:

- Generally speaking, you can't change a court order by simple agreement. In almost every circumstance, only a court order can vary or alter an existing court order.

- If the instrument that needs to be changed is an agreement, you can probably effect a change to that agreement provided the change is properly recorded in writing in the same manner as the agreement itself. Again, jurisdictional variations may mean agreements will require different levels of formality, but it is almost invariably true that an agreement can be modified by a subsequent agreement that's written, properly witnessed, and so on.

- It is a bad idea to attempt to vary a written agreement by way of a further oral agreement. If you want to change a written agreement, do it in writing, and describe it as a variation or amendment to the original. Keep both the original and the amendment. If you're unsure about any aspect of the process, consult a professional.

- When you make an amendment, explain the reason. Be simple and clear. For instance, the recital portion of the amending agreement (near the beginning) should say something like this: "The parties to this amending agreement wish to vary their original agreement because Bob's income has increased significantly. As a result, they have agreed to vary the child support terms which they had previously settled upon in 2009, by the following … "

- In the amending agreement, use the same language, terms, and names that have been used in the original agreement. If you call the support "maintenance" in the first agreement, don't suddenly call it "alimony" or "support" in the amending agreement. Continue to call it "maintenance" so that there's no confusion.

- Do not purport to revoke the original agreement if your intention is only to vary one or two parts or provisions. Instead, include a clause that says, "The parties agree that because their son Todd is now attending college, this amending agreement is needed to adjust the provisions describing the child support payable by the husband to the wife. This amending agreement is intended to explain how they will share

Todd's college expenses. In all other respects, their original agreement made October 10, 2009, shall continue to govern except as varied herein."

- If the change that is needed is contentious, do not throw the baby out with the bath water. If you and your spouse settled matters previously, but are now facing a one- or two-issue speed bump, don't panic, and do not suggest that the original agreement should be set aside. You solved your issues once before, and you can probably do it again. Remain committed to the process that resulted in problem-solving success previously, and try to negotiate an amendment. If you cannot, get help, but do not suggest that all bets are off.

- Don't change the original agreement every time there's a minor modification to your arrangement. Many parents are able to fine-tune access arrangements from time to time without actually rewriting their contract every few months. Keep in mind that there is some elasticity in any agreement, and periodic and incidental adjustments may not require formalization.

An example of a change that should be recorded in writing is any major change to custody or support. Examples of changes that may form part of a written variation would include a one-time agreement to pay for some special event or expense (e.g., a child's ski lessons or dental surgery), or a periodic adjustment to access (e.g., the pick-up time will change from 5:00 p.m. to 5:30 p.m. every Wednesday).

In some high conflict families, it's indeed necessary to document every change imaginable, but if you've purchased this book, you're probably not part of that group. Use common sense. Minor changes can be made without written proof. Major changes should be properly recorded. It's a question of degree.

12

Update Your Will

Where I live and work, there are some strict and often misunderstood rules about wills and separation. The governing law at the present time is that a marriage revokes an existing will unless the will is made in specific contemplation of marriage (and says so). So, in almost all cases, when you marry, your will becomes void, useless, and powerless.

However, when you separate and divorce, your will is not automatically void. Unless you do something to revoke your will, it continues to govern long after separation. These rules may or may not prevail where you reside, but in my jurisdiction they offer fertile ground for lawsuits of all kinds.

Regardless of the actual state of law in your area, it's always wise (and in fact, probably imperative) to reconsider your estate plans whenever there is a material change in your wealth or your status as a spouse or parent. That means that you should look at, read, and understand your will every time you marry, have a child, or end a durable romantic relationship (and by that, I mean any relationship in which you have arguably cohabited for more than a year). No one is going to force you to do so, but it's wise. If you do not consider the matter and ensure that your will is valid and accurately reflects your prevailing testamentary wishes, you may be leaving nothing to your heirs, or you may be leaving something worse: the prospect of estate litigation.

If you have separated, and are satisfied that your heirs (usually your children) are properly provided for, you may not need to make a change. Most married parties, however, have mirror wills, in which each spouse says that all his or her worldly goods shall pass to the surviving spouse on death. After separation, that's probably no longer appropriate.

Note that if you intend to leave assets or income to children, they will need a legal guardian or trustee to administer the inheritance in the event that you die before the children reach the age of majority.

Obviously, it's not necessary to rewrite a will if you're simply thinking about separating, or if you remain satisfied that, in the event of death, your spouse or former spouse should have your assets. It's also not necessary to hire counsel to review your will every time your daughter enrols in college or your son moves out. It is, however, wise to keep a copy of your last testament handy, and to review it regularly to ensure that it continues to fairly allocate your estate in the event of your demise. In the event of separation, read your will and ask yourself if it satisfactorily provides for the friends and family for whom you care.

As we know, horrible and unexpected things happen all the time. Having a current and valid will on file at all times is smart, and it might save your survivors thousands of dollars and plenty of anguish.

Remember, too, that in many jurisdictions (such as mine), the court maintains a residual power or capacity to vary an unfair will. Although this legislation is not yet widespread, there are similar laws in many places throughout North America.

This law (in British Columbia, called the *Wills Variation Act*), invites the court to intervene and rewrite or modify a will which fails to fairly provide for a spouse or children. Although the court seems to have a largely unbridled power of review, in practice, judges show some deference to the principle that, generally speaking, a testator's wishes are to be respected.

That won't happen, however, where a nasty will-writer "cut out" a child or spouse, particularly for improper reasons. For example, a son who was disinherited because he was gay had his share of his father's estate repaid to him at trial because the court found the testator's reason for disinheriting unjust.

In other cases, a testator who favored a church or charity over his or her own offspring had the will varied by the court. Sometimes, the successful litigant is an adult child (occasionally even a mistreated or disadvantaged and truly deserving child), but the law applies equally to spouses. In my jurisdiction, a spouse includes a common-law lover in which the relationship has endured for more than two years.

This law, in the view of many, makes good sense. It encourages testators to be fair, sensible, and just in disposing of their assets. It does not require parents to give everything to their children absolutely and equally, but it does mean that in cases in which surviving spouses and children are disadvantaged, there's accountability. For the government, this makes good sense too. These laws mean that no nasty testator can disinherit a needy child and download the financial responsibility for his or her survivors to the state — if the estate has assets, those assets may be distributed amongst the needy family members, despite what the testator wanted.

If the children are all adults, independent, and not disadvantaged, there's little likelihood that a court will interfere with a proper estate plan that fairly allocates the resources in accordance with the testator's wishes. There is, quite clearly, nothing wrong with a parent providing a little more or a little less to one child over another, by reason of commitment, devotion, need, or other factors (sometimes known only to the testator). The *Wills Variation Act* does not require equality, only fairness where support or maintenance is at issue.

In any event, the purpose of this book is not to argue the wisdom of such laws, or to convince readers that variation laws are good or bad. The point here is merely this: Wills are important. They are your opportunity to distribute your assets (your legacy) amongst the people and institutions who will remain after you are gone.

If you don't have a will, you need to get one. There is simply no excuse for having no will (unless you truly have no assets, no debts, no children, and no lover). If you do have a will, it has no value unless it is current and accurate. Keep your will handy, and review it often to ensure that it truly reflects your testamentary desires. Get legal advice about the will and the provisions you make for your heirs.

Finally, even if there's no wills legislation in your area now, know that there may be some day. Even if that never comes to pass in your jurisdiction, your will really should be fair, and should allocate your legacy in a reasonable way amongst your survivors.

Resources

Throughout this book, I have encouraged readers to take personal responsibility for gathering information about their legal issues. I have suggested that with the resources that are available online, in libraries, and through other resource centers, there is really no excuse for not being informed.

In most urban areas, there is good, current, and inexpensive or free information that's readily available. Often, the data you want and need is accessible through a local bar (lawyer's) association or group, or from a university or college, or from one of many societies that offer support to litigants and parents who are willing to reach out for help. These organizations are easy to find online, and are often accessible by toll free telephone. Chances are that if you live in a big city and cannot find help, you're not looking in the right places. If that's so, talk to a local lawyer, or spend time at the library or on the Internet until you do get what you need.

For people who reside in rural or remote areas, the challenge can be greater. If you find it difficult to access justice information because you live far away from a major metropolitan center, I suggest that you find resource services online and be industrious. Call the nearest urban center or university and explain your circumstance, and tell them that you are in need of help. If all else fails, call the nearest lawyer and ask him or her for the numbers of the local bar association and the state or provincial law society.

Another good resource for parties needing general legal information about family law is the site for the national bar associations. The websites for the American Bar Association and the Canadian Bar Association are massive central information hubs that can be very helpful, and will offer referrals to other sites and resources.

I have, in this section, avoided recommending other books, websites, and resources for specific and deliberate reasons. There are several reasons I refrain from doing so:

- While the information in this book is general and designed to help readers fashion an approach to their family law problems, most published books offer specific and substantive legal advice. That advice can become aged (and wrong) very quickly, and may do more harm than good as a result. It would be unwise for me to recommend specific texts to any reader because, for the most part, these references will soon be out of date and probably irrelevant relatively quickly.

- While there are many excellent resources in the legal information market, there are also, quite frankly, many poorly researched and inadequate publications that are dangerously inaccurate. Worse still, most of the information is regionally sensitive. In the end, the adage "a little knowledge is a dangerous thing" often rings true, so I am personally unhappy about endorsing any other author. Besides, a properly crafted book about Florida family law may be fine for a Florida resident, but would be completely inadequate for someone living in Ontario.

- Until you have gathered some knowledge about your problem, and done at least a little general research, you probably won't know exactly which issues you need or want more information about — the topics you need to know and understand may be quite unimaginable when you start your study.

- As you work your way through the myriad of available resources, remember that while some of the information on the Internet is very interesting and helpful, a fair portion of it is just plain wrong. You are less likely to get bad advice or information from a local lawyer or bar association, but again, remember that you get what you pay for. A free initial consultation can be comforting and informative, but it's unlikely to solve your problems. Moreover, remember my advice that no matter what happens, you simply must see a lawyer to review any document or agreement *before* you sign it.

In the first few drafts of this book I closed my writing with the comment "good luck." On review, however, I have decided that luck has no place in the process, so that's an inappropriate comment. Instead, I will say only this: If you are separating, try your best to negotiate a sensible resolution. Start by remembering that litigation really is not an alternative.

Remember, a negotiated compromise is the only way to truly ensure a happy divorce.

OTHER TITLES OF INTEREST FROM
Self·Counsel Press

Separation Agreement
David Greig
ISBN: 978-1-55180-789-8
$24.95 CAD

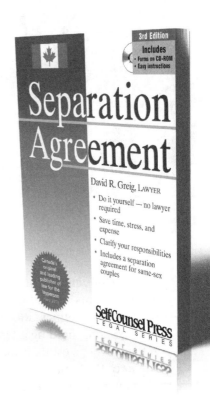

When married Canadians choose to live apart, each has certain rights and obligations that can be settled by an agreement — or be determined by the courts. *Separation Agreement* is designed to help avoid litigation over family assets, maintenance, and custody by helping couples address the issues and write down their agreement in a clear and concise manner. It's written by a lawyer and is easy to use. This kit contains the following:

- Save time, stress, and expense

- Face the future with certainty

- Clarify your responsibilities

A CD-ROM contains the blank separation agreement form in Word (6.0 or higher) and PDF formats for use on a Windows-based PC. Also included is an agreement that same-sex couples can use. Note: **Legal in all Canadian provinces except Quebec.**

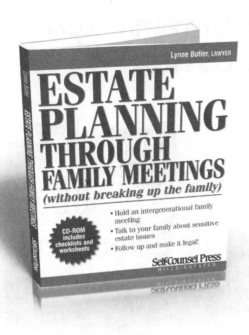

Estate Planning through Family Meetings

Lynne Butler

ISBN: 978-1-77040-036-8

$23.95 USD/$24.95 CAD

Estate planning and writing a will are among the last things families want to think about, and yet they are so important. Perhaps you want to ensure that your parents have their affairs in order before they pass away, but you probably don't want to bring it up and risk upsetting them or looking greedy.

Estate Planning through Family Meetings (without breaking up the family) presents an easier way to handle estate planning: through a process of meetings and notetaking. As author and lawyer Lynne Butler explains, holding a family meeting to discuss what should happen to a parent's estate is an effective method, because it allows each member of the family to talk openly, ask questions, and work together, so that everyone feels they've had their say.

Using the steps outlined in the book, the author shows you how to plan ahead, hold meetings with your family, learn how to document an estate plan, and make it legal. She covers the issues you'll need to be aware of to do it properly, the legal consequences of insufficient planning, and how to deal with special circumstances such as family businesses, cottages, and trusts.

The book includes a CD-ROM for use on a Windows-based PC, loaded with checklists and tools to help the process along and ensure nothing is forgotten.